Lithuanian History

A Captivating Guide to the Ancient Prussians and Samogitians, the Grand Duchy of Lithuania, Soviet Occupation, and Modern Times

© Copyright 2025 - All rights reserved.

The content contained within this book may not be reproduced, duplicated, or transmitted without direct written permission from the author or the publisher.

Under no circumstances will any blame or legal responsibility be held against the publisher, or author, for any damages, reparation, or monetary loss due to the information contained within this book, either directly or indirectly.

Legal Notice:

This book is copyright protected. It is only for personal use. You cannot amend, distribute, sell, use, quote, or paraphrase any part, or the content within this book, without the consent of the author or publisher.

Disclaimer Notice:

Please note the information contained within this document is for educational and entertainment purposes only. All effort has been executed to present accurate, up-to-date, reliable, and complete information. No warranties of any kind are declared or implied. Readers acknowledge that the author is not engaging in the rendering of legal, financial, medical, or professional advice. The content within this book has been derived from various sources. Please consult a licensed professional before attempting any techniques outlined in this book.

By reading this document, the reader agrees that under no circumstances is the author responsible for any losses, direct or indirect, that are incurred as a result of the use of the information contained within this document, including, but not limited to, errors, omissions, or inaccuracies.

Free Bonus from Captivating History (Available for a Limited time)

Hi History Lovers!

Now you have a chance to join our exclusive history list so you can get your first history ebook for free as well as discounts and a potential to get more history books for free!

Simply visit the link below to join.

Or, Scan the QR code!

captivatinghistory.com/ebook

Also, make sure to follow us on Facebook, X, and YouTube by searching for Captivating History.

Table of Contents

INTRODUCTION 1
CHAPTER ONE – THE BLOODY BIRTH OF LITHUANIA 3
CHAPTER TWO – THE CRUSADES AND THE RISE OF THE DUCHY OF LITHUANIA 12
CHAPTER THREE – LIFE AND DEATH STRUGGLES WITH THE CRUSADERS 20
CHAPTER FOUR – FROM PAGANISM TO CHRISTIANITY AND FROM DUCHY TO COMMONWEALTH 28
CHAPTER FIVE – WARS WITH RUSSIA AND THE UNION OF LUBLIN (1430-1570) 37
CHAPTER SIX – THE POLISH-LITHUANIAN COMMONWEALTH: RISE AND FALL (1569-1778) 46
CHAPTER SEVEN – FROM RUSSIAN TYRANNY TO INDEPENDENCE 56
CHAPTER EIGHT – HITLER, STALIN, AND THE HOLOCAUST 66
CHAPTER NINE – SOVIET TERROR AND REPRESSION POST-WWII (1944-1985) 75
CHAPTER TEN – OPPORTUNITIES AND OLD THREATS 84
CONCLUSION 92
HERE'S ANOTHER BOOK BY CAPTIVATING HISTORY THAT YOU MIGHT LIKE 95
FREE BONUS FROM CAPTIVATING HISTORY (AVAILABLE FOR A LIMITED TIME) 96
BIBLIOGRAPHY 97
IMAGE SOURCES 98

Introduction

Lithuania has a fascinating and turbulent history that is little known or understood. It is a story of war, empire-building, and the struggle for freedom. Did you know Lithuania was the last pagan country in Europe, fought Christian Crusaders, and was also the most significant European state for a time? Even today, the country plays an important role in global affairs. This tiny nation stands at one of the crossroads of Europe and has historically been the home of many people groups. Understanding Lithuania allows us to understand better the history of Eastern Europe, Russia, Germany, and the Jews. In this book, you will learn about pagan warlords, the Mongols, and freedom fighters, such as the Lithuanian Joan of Arc.

Lithuanian history is an exciting story and, at times, a tragic one. This work narrates the history of Lithuania from ancient times and the emergence of its unique Baltic society and culture to the time of the Northern Crusades. Lithuania remained pagan, and as a result, its people had to endure attacks by Christian Crusaders who sought to convert them and take their lands. This book details how the Lithuanians managed to remain independent and staunchly pagan until well into the Middle Ages.

They not only survived; they also managed to create an empire. By the 15th century, the Duchy of Lithuania was the largest in Europe. Lithuania eventually became Christianized when its rulers became the kings of Poland. The Polish-Lithuanian Commonwealth played a decisive role in eastern Europe, including defeating the Mongols and holding back the Ottoman Turks. Lithuania was once prosperous, enlightened, and diverse, with Catholic and Orthodox Christians, Muslims, and Jews. Indeed, during the 18th century, Lithuania became one of Judaism's most important religious and intellectual centers.

The Commonwealth of Poland and Lithuania eventually fell into decline and suffered multiple invasions. In the late 18th century, the Russians occupied the nation. The country fought to regain its freedom and retain its national identity. The Lithuanians regained their independence after World War I. This was not to last, though, as it was occupied by the Soviet Union and then Nazi Germany. Lithuania's Jewish population was exterminated during the Holocaust.

After the defeat of the Nazis, the Lithuanians again suffered repression from Stalin. This book offers a detailed discussion of the little-known fight for independence by the Brothers of the Forest Lithuanian partisans. Lithuania's resistance to Sovietization and the eradication of its national identity are also talked about. The country became the first to break free of the Soviet Union and helped to contribute to its ultimate demise. You will also discover modern Lithuania's role in the Russo-Ukrainian War and why the country is a champion of democracy and freedom today.

There is so much to unpack when discussing Lithuanian history and its fight for freedom. This introductory book is meant to serve as a stepping stone for future research into this enthralling country and region. To begin, let's take a look at the early origins of Lithuania.

Chapter One – The Bloody Birth of Lithuania

Geography and Origins

The modern Republic of Lithuania is one of the three Baltic republics in northeast Europe. Today, it borders Poland, Belarus, Kaliningrad (an exclave of the Russian Federation), and Latvia.

Geography has always been crucial in the development of any country or region. Lithuania, or in the native language, Lietuvos, is situated on the eastern Baltic Sea. The land is relatively flat, and there is no significant mountain range, although highlands in the east form a natural barrier. This is a result of the last ice age when the country was under gigantic icebergs. Many swamps and small lakes mark the landscape, and in the past, dense forests covered much of the terrain. Even today, it is estimated that one-third of the land is covered by forests. The area has limited natural resources but had (and still has) reasonable agricultural land. This means that Lithuania has always been sparsely populated apart from the coast and that its lands produced hardy and independent individuals. Despite the often-difficult terrain, Lithuania was always a crossroads for east and west and north and south, and it was influential in trade and cultural exchange.

The area's first attested inhabitants in what is now known as Lithuania were hunter-gatherers after the last ice age. These people appear to have come from the southwest (modern Poland) and the east (Russia). These hunter-gatherers began to settle down and eventually adopted agriculture. Genetic research has shown that, unlike the rest of northern Europe, the hunter-gatherers did not intermarry with the wave of Anatolian immigrants who brought agriculture to the region.

In the 4th millennium, the Indo-Europeans arrived in the area. By the 1st century CE, the territory of what is now Lithuania was peopled by the Balts. The Balts are an ethno-linguistic group that speaks one of the Baltic languages, which are also known to linguists as Balto-Slavic. This family of languages is noted for the conservative and archaic features of their language. In the early years of the Common Era (CE), the Germanic tribes' domination of eastern Europe appears to have isolated the ancestors of the Lithuanians. The collapse of the Western Roman Empire, which resulted in the Germanic tribes moving into Roman lands, eased the pressure on the Balts and allowed them to preserve their ancient ways and language.

Around 600 CE, the Balts covered a large area of what is now northeastern Europe and even settled in what is now Russia. The so-called Dnieper Balts lived in what is now Ukraine. They were divided into many tribes and were remarkably diverse. During the Early Middle Ages, they became divided into the Western Balts, such as the ancient Prussians, and the Eastern Balts, such as the Samogitians. The Lithuanians are believed to be descended from the Eastern Balts. Many Balts assimilated with the Slavs, but the forebearers of the Lithuanians were isolated because of their geography. Because of its geographical features, Lithuania was not encroached upon by invaders, allowing it to preserve its own culture. Dense forests meant that wood was freely available. Many early wooden buildings, such as temples, did not survive because of near-constant war and because they were constructed of wood. We do not have a good impression of the material culture of the inhabitants of medieval Lithuania.

The Amber Road

In the classical period, Lithuania was one of the key areas in the lucrative amber trade. Amber is a form of fossilized resin and can be gold or yellow in color. It can be worked in various forms and is regarded as a semi-precious stone. Copious amounts have been found in the tombs of ancient Greeks and Romans. There was a massive demand for this material for centuries.

Modern historians have developed the theory of the Amber Road. This route was where amber and other goods were sent down the Vistula and other rivers to the Mediterranean and beyond. The Mediterranean nations exported metal and other luxury goods to the Baltic area in exchange for this material. As a result of this, the local Balts, including the forebearers of the Lithuanians, grew rich. In Roman times, the main route began in Lithuania, and amber was transported from its coastline by river to the Roman Empire. Amber remained important in the Lithuanian economy, and local artisans became skilled in making amber ornaments, a tradition that continues today.

According to classical sources, modern-day Lithuania was inhabited by the tribes known collectively as the Yotvingians or Galindians. In the Early Middle Ages, the eastern Baltic area was inhabited by five major groups. An interesting fact is that the modern Latvians are closely related to the Lithuanians, and they are the last remnants of the once-widespread Balts.

Lithuanian tribes.[1]

Ancient Tribes and Vikings

The various Baltic tribes were quite different. There were distinct differences between the Aukštaitai, who lived in the uplands, and the Samogitians, who lived in the swampy lowlands. While there were undoubtedly differences, the tribes shared cultural similarities. Scholars believe they retained features of both the language and culture of their Indo-European ancestors. The Balts had a reputation as fierce warriors. Every man had to be a warrior. The tribes were ruled by a warlord, and clan allegiance was important. This warrior culture was essential, as the first Lithuanians faced threats from all quarters, including the Slavs and especially the Vikings. It is probable that many Lithuanians served with the Vikings when they were not fighting them.

Historians accept that a shared religion and culture united several distinct Lithuanian tribal groups in the early medieval period. Among the tribes that later merged to form the historic Lithuanian people are the Aukštaitai, Sudovians, Old Prussians, Curonians, Semigallians, Selonians, Skalvians, Yotvingians, and Samogitians. These groups often played an essential part in the politics of northeastern Europe. At times, they were often obliged to pay tribute to stronger groups, especially the Vikings, but they were never conquered, thanks to their warrior ethos and their rough terrain.

The Curonians gained a reputation as fearsome pirates and fighters, and it is even claimed that they raided or even invaded what is now Sweden. They eventually gave their name to the historic area known as Courland. The Semigallians were also noted warriors and are believed to have defeated an army of Swedish Vikings who sought to control a key trade route. The Sudovians, another group of proto-Lithuanians, are known to have served as mercenaries in Kievan Rus', the state that eventually gave rise to Ukraine and Russia. The Skalvians established a large wooden castle that dominated trade routes along the Neman River.

Another group that played an important part in the emergence of the modern Lithuanians is the Samogitians. There is some dispute as to whether they were Lithuanians or a subset. Samogitian is considered a dialect of Lithuanian, and it is still widely spoken today.

All the tribes farmed the land, fished the rivers and sea, and traded goods, mostly by river. They had extensive dealings with Scandinavians, the Slavic peoples of what became Russia, and the Finno-Ugric peoples. Lithuanians not only became distinct from the Western Balts but also from their fellow Eastern Balts. Linguists believe that the Lithuanian and Latvian languages diverged in the 8th century CE.

In the Early Middle Ages, the people who lived in what is now Lithuania had an oral culture, and they kept no written records. Their history was handed down through stories and poems. This means that our knowledge of the early history of the first Lithuanians is fragmentary. However, they had a vibrant culture, and they even assimilated many Uralic peoples related to the modern Finns and Hungarians.

The religion of the Balts and the early Lithuanians is poorly recorded. Yet, religion played a crucial role in the early development of the Eastern Balts. It is accepted that the Lithuanians were among the last people, if not the last, to be Christianized in Europe. The persistence of paganism shaped their culture and the emergence of a distinct identity. Their resistance to Christianity meant they became assimilated by other large groups.

The Old Balt religion has many similarities to the ancient religion of the Indo-Europeans. Some scholars see similarities between it and the Indian and Iranian traditions. As noted above, the Balts were a conservative culture, and scholars have studied them for the insights they reveal about the ancient Indo-European culture. The Balts believed the world was divided into two or three regions and that it always existed. The sun tree was at the center of the world, while the gods resided in the sky mountain.

One of the most important gods in the Baltic pantheon was the sun, a feminine deity that is portrayed as both a daughter and a mother. Dievas is the main male deity and is often associated with Jupiter and Zeus in classical mythology. He is the father of the other sky gods and is associated with the family and the farm. In Baltic mythology, he is married to the sun, and the other gods are their children. Perkons was the god of thunder and storms and was feared. Mēness was the god of the moon, and he was also the god of war. In East Baltic mythology, there was also a devil and werewolves. There was a plethora of underworld, forest, and agricultural deities, and they often had a local cult. Another feature of the religion was that many households kept sacred grass snakes.

Based on sources such as the later clerical accounts, a pagan priesthood still existed. There were augurs and sorcerers, but most religious functions were conducted by the heads of clans or families.

They performed rituals and had immense prestige. This close connection between family and religion allowed paganism to flourish even after Lithuania had become Christian. As late as the 18th century, Christian clergymen complained of sorcerers, who were esteemed by the local people, having the audacity to practice diabolical rites. Scholars have argued that there were centralized places of worship, which gave the disparate clans and families, who often lived in isolated homesteads, a sense of collective identity.

The traditional religion has the features of a natural religion, and the Lithuanians remain deeply attached to nature even to this day. This close attachment to the land, like the Native Americans in the United States, meant they fought hard for their native land.

Women in pagan Lithuania had a high status. They could own and inherit property. Women played a crucial role in marriage alliances and religious life as priestesses. Many females worked on farms and had a significant role in the agricultural sector. Many generations of women lived in the same household. Divorce was common, and polygamy was also practiced by the elite. Women were constantly at risk of being abducted by raiders. Numerous females, especially captives, endured a life of slavery or became concubines in medieval Lithuanian society.

The First Lithuanians

In the 11th century, the first mention of the Lithuanian tribe (Litua) was made in a German chronicle. The origin of the name is controversial, but researchers believe that it might have been based on a river and indicates the geographical origin of the tribe.

They were a small and powerless tribe, and their ethnogenesis is uncertain. They slowly grew in power, and other tribes turned to them for defense from the constant Viking raids. The Lithuanians at this stage only occupied a small portion of what would become the future medieval state and were distinct from the other tribes that were to form the Lithuanian nation.

The early Lithuanians seemed to have developed an elaborate war machine. For much of the 11th century, the lands of what is now Lithuania were constantly ravaged, especially by the Slavic Ruthenians. This led to the emergence of the proto-Lithuanian state centered on Aukštaitija, which is in the northern uplands and one of the five historic territories of Lithuania. This was the first state established by any of the Balts.

By the late 11th century, the Lithuanian tribe had become so powerful that they went on the offensive. Their actions would form the basis of the future Lithuanian state. They began to raid their neighbors, including the Ruthenians and even the Rus'. During these raids, they collected wealth and enslaved prisoners. As a result, there was pressure on the tribal society, which had been based on clans and families and was democratic, with leaders only having limited power. As the Lithuanian tribe became more powerful, a powerful warrior class emerged, and it came to dominate society. This led to social tensions. Oftentimes, the Lithuanian tribes fought and subdued other related tribes that became part of the Lithuanian state.

Despite the success of the Lithuanians, they and the other tribes were at times obliged to pay tribute to the Kingdom of Denmark. Denmark was a powerful mercantile and naval power. It used the paganism of the Baltic peoples as an excuse to seize their lands. Several Danish kings had ambitions to establish an empire in the eastern Baltic. The need to pay the Danes tribute in the early 11th century led to more Lithuanian state-building. In 1219, the Danes launched a crusade against neighboring tribes in what is now Lithuania. They retained outposts in the Baltic until the early modern period.

More important for the future of Lithuania was the great German eastward migration. The German lands experienced a demographic boom in the High Middle Ages, and industry and trade expanded. Around one thousand German settlers crossed the Elbe River and established towns and farms in Slavic and Baltic lands. By 1200, there were small German outposts in what is now Lithuania, which was the beginning of centuries of often bitter relations between Germans and Lithuanians.

Age of the Crusaders

The High Middle Ages was also the Age of the Crusaders. Christian kingdoms under the spiritual leadership of the pope believed they had a duty to defend Christians and to Christianize those who refused to follow the teachings of the Catholic Church. In the 11th century, western European Crusaders invaded the Middle East to retake the holy city of Jerusalem. After succeeding in this, they established Crusader States that tried to defy the Muslims until the end of the 13th century.

By the early 13th century, the German, Polish, and Scandinavian rulers were all Christians, and they believed they had a religious duty to convert their pagan neighbors who followed polytheistic beliefs. These rulers undertook forays to conquer the non-Christians, motivated by a desire to Christianize pagans and seize new lands. For example, the Germans conquered and colonized the Slavic Wends during their crusade in what is now eastern Germany. The 1190s saw the beginning of the Northern Crusades, a concentrated campaign by European rulers to Christianize and colonize the last pagans in northeast Europe. By the early 13th century, the Crusaders had Christianized modern Finland and eastern Germany. They then turned their attention to the pagan Balts who lived on important trade routes. The Crusaders wanted these people to accept Catholicism, not the rival Orthodox Christian faith. In 1202, a German bishop in what is now Latvia established the crusading order of the Livonian Sword Brothers, which consisted of warrior monks.

Later, Holy Roman Emperor Frederick II issued a bull that tasked the military monks with subjugating the pagan Balts. The rationale behind this was that only monks with a religious vocation would be committed to engaging in the Christianization of stubborn pagans in the vast forests and marshes. They often forcefully converted the people of Livonia (modern Latvia).

In 1208, the Livonian Sword Brothers, nearly all Germans, began a crusade with the king of Denmark against the people who now live in Estonia. This was a long and brutal campaign, and Lithuanian tribes, such as the Cournians, became involved and sided with their fellow Balts. During this crusade, the Selonians, another early Lithuanian people, came under attack from the German warrior monks. By 1224, Estonia was under Crusader control, at least nominally, but the subjugated people regularly rebelled.

The Teutonic Knights: Fearsome Warrior Monks

Around 1191, the Teutonic Order was founded as an order of military monks. At first, the order served in the Kingdom of Jerusalem until its fall and later in Hungary, but after they were expelled from this kingdom, they were given the authority to launch a crusade against the Old Prussians, a Western Baltic people who gave their name to the future state of Prussia. Beginning in the 1220s, the German warrior monks launched regular raids against the Old Prussians and gradually wore them down as they seized more of their lands. The Teutonic Order established an independent state out of conquered lands. This laid the foundation of Prussia. By 1225, Lithuania was flanked by the

Livonian Sword Brothers to the north and the Teutonic Order to the west. Both the crusading orders at this stage operated independently of each other.

In 1226, the Livonian Sword Brothers attacked the Samogitians, a Lithuanian tribe and one of the fiercest enemies of the Crusaders. The Livonian Order launched a raid into Samogitian territory, but on their return journey home, the Samogitians ambushed them on some marshy ground in what came to be called the Battle of Saule. The lightly armed Samogitians threw lances at the heavy-mounted German knights. By the end of the battle, numerous knights of the Livonian Sword Brothers had died, including the order's master, and the order had been virtually destroyed. The pope reconstituted the Livonian Sword Brothers as the Livonian Order and placed them under the authority of the larger Teutonic Order.

The area governed by the early Lithuanian state escaped the Crusaders' wrath and continued to build its strength. Its rulers knew that it was only a matter of time before the Germans or Danes launched an attack, and this instigated a series of events that resulted in the Grand Duchy of Lithuania, which sought to maintain the independence of the last free and pagan Balts.

Chapter Two – The Crusades and the Rise of the Duchy of Lithuania

Forged in War: The Emergence of the Grand Duchy

The genesis of the Duchy of Lithuania is poorly attested. The local powerful lords came together due to the increased Crusader threat. They were known as dukes, and the leaders became known as senior dukes. Each of the lesser dukes held a great deal of autonomy and power within their domains. It was not so much a duchy as a confederation of tribes and clans. They came together to raid their enemies and to defend their territories and those of their allies. Based on the archaeological evidence, the Lithuanian lords and nobility had fortifications built in the woods and marshes and grew rich on trade and raiding.

The year 1209 is widely seen as the beginning of what became known as the Grand Duchy of Lithuania. In this year, written chronicles and records became available. There was one senior duke and subordinate dukes who represented various tribes. They all came together in an alliance of mutual defense and collaborated with each other. They entered a peace treaty with the Ruthenians.

We know some of the names of the dukes. The first that we know of was Žvelgaitis, who was killed in a raid on Riga (Livonia). His successor, Daugirutis, was powerful enough to enter into relations with the wealthy Novgorod city-state in what is now northern Russia. He was captured during a raid on Livonia and killed himself in prison. His successor was also killed in a raid.

The nascent Lithuanian dukedom went into a period of decline after this, and the Samogitians and other Lithuanian tribes acted independently with no centralized leadership. However, after 1217, the small Lithuanian state or duchy was far from helpless against the encroachment of warrior monks and German colonists. It was a small, aggressive state that raided the lands of its neighbors, including the Rus' and the Poles. Every year, the Lithuanian heavy and light cavalry raided lands, seizing plunder and captives. The Lithuanian cavalry and light infantry became famous and could fight on a range of battlefields, unlike their enemies. They were to lay the foundations of an empire.

The Coming of the Mongols

One of the senior dukes, Mindaugas, is believed to have come to dominate the Lithuanian polity by 1236, if not earlier. We know little about his early life and how he came to power. He was a successful war leader who made shrewd political marriages to build his power. Mindaugas was ruthless and regularly murdered his rivals.

Woodcut of Mindaugas from the 17th century by Alexander Guagnini.[2]

In the aftermath of the defeat of the Livonians at the Battle of Saule, the Lithuanians under Mindaugas exploited the situation in the former Kievan Rus' lands. Kievan Rus' had ruled much of what is now European Russia and Ukraine, but in 1240, Kiev (today's Kyiv) had been sacked by mounted warriors from the east. These warriors were the Mongols.

While the Lithuanians were state-building, integrating other tribes that were culturally related into their nascent duchy, many of their kinsmen, such as the Samogitians, remained independent. By 1240, the German Teutonic Order controlled what is now Kaliningrad and Estonia directly and indirectly. The knights had taken holy orders, but they were an elite fighting force. They also had a corps of crossbowmen considered among the best in Europe. They established a colonial state dominated by Germans in Prussia in the name of Christianity. The reconstituted Livonian Order of warrior monks, with the support of the Teutonic Order, was instructed to subdue and Christianize the heathen Lithuanians, who were capable fighters but still largely divided along tribal lines.

After the Battle of Saule, the Livonian Order was too weak, which allowed the Lithuanians to build up their strength. They actively helped the pagan Prussians in their fight against the Teutonic Order, and they engaged in raids on lands held by the German military order. The Teutonic Order waged an almost genocidal war against the Prussians. It was a war of raids and counterraids. The Germans burned unfortified villages and crops and took slaves so that they could be converted to Christianity.

Around 1239, the nascent Duchy of Lithuania met the people who inspired fear in everyone. The dreaded Mongols had destroyed Kievan Rus', and most of their surviving princes became the tributaries of Genghis Khan's descendants. Annoyed by Lithuanian raids, a Mongolian army with cohorts of Rus' soldiers advanced on Lithuanian territory and raided it. There is no doubt they devastated the land. They also raided and despoiled the lands of the neighboring Yotvingians.

Lithuania was lucky that it did not suffer the same fate as the other people that the Mongols had conquered. Nevertheless, they had to endure sporadic raids from the Mongols. There is some debate as to whether the Lithuanians became the tributaries of the Golden Horde, the Mongolian dynasty that came to rule Russia. They might have briefly become tributaries, but the Lithuanians soon began to raid territory that was directly or indirectly controlled by the Mongols, especially in Ruthenia, which is now Ukraine and Belarus. This suggests that the Lithuanians, unlike their neighbors, remained independent.

The Mongols defeated the Teutonic Order and the Poles, which allowed the Lithuanians a respite. They continued to expand and develop alliances. Nevertheless, the military orders and German settlers in Kurland (Estonia) continued to pressure the Lithuanians, which encouraged them to expand to the southeast. In the 1240s, the important Slavic Principality of Polotsk became a vassal of the Lithuanians.

Mindaugas's rule was successful; he had resisted the Mongols and the Crusaders and had even expanded Lithuanian territory. However, the Lithuanian elite was divided by feuds and disputes that often led to fighting. Mindaugas was phenomenally successful in his state-building efforts, but he overextended himself when he tried to seize the lands of his nephews. They formed a powerful coalition with other disaffected nobles and the Galicians (modern western Ukraine). Mindaugas was unable to resist, and it seemed as if he would lose his control over the duchy. He decided to do something unthinkable. Mindaugas traveled to Riga and accepted baptism. At the same time, the Livonian Order began to raid Lithuania. With the help of a unit of Livonian crossbowmen, Mindaugas was able to take back much of his lands and defeat the coalition. In 1250, a major Mongolian invasion ordered by Berke Khan to secure the submission of the Lithuanians weakened Mindaugas's enemies and strengthened his hand.

The First Lithuanian Kingdom

By 1251, Mindaugas had reasserted his control over most of Lithuania and its vassal lands. He conceded territories to the Livonians and his rivals, such as Daniel of Galicia. A series of papal bulls established an ecclesiastical structure in Lithuania, and work began on the first cathedral in Vilnius. Mindaugas's family and followers received the sacrament of baptism alongside Mindaugas. He was crowned king of Lithuania in 1253. This brought Lithuanians into Christendom and revolutionized the geopolitical situation in the eastern Baltic.

The first Lithuanian king achieved some significant peace agreements. The strongholds and hill forts of the Lithuanians began to resemble towns filled with religious orders, traders, and merchants. However, Berke Khan of the Golden Horde was worried by the growing strength of the Lithuanians and by the conversion of the state to Christianity. He sent a large army of Mongolian cavalrymen, horse archers, and vassals. Many of these vassals also owed allegiance to Mindaugas. As usual, the Mongols ravaged the lands with horrific efficiency, but Mindaugas's core lands escaped the worst of it once again.

Mindaugas had converted to Catholicism, but Orthodox Christianity was also influential in his lands. His son became an Orthodox monk.

Battle of Durbe and Aftermath

In 1252, the Livonian Order established a castle at Klaipėda, which became known as Memel in German. The Samogitians and Lithuanians, especially their merchants, resented this. Samogitia was culturally Lithuanian but not part of the kingdom at this time. The Livonian Order's rule in the region was heavy-handed, leading to outright conflict. At the Battle of Skuodas in 1259, the Samogitians defeated the Livonian Order, killing dozens of knights. These knights were critical to the order, as they often won battles alone. The prowess of the knights was crucial since the Crusaders were numerically inferior to the Balts.

Skuodas was a disaster for the Livonian Order, and the Teutonic Order had to hastily send reinforcements to Livonia. They were later joined by some Danes. The military orders invaded Samogitia in 1260, but the Samogitians began to raid Courland. The German Crusaders had to turn back to defend Courland but were ambushed by the Samogitians at Durbe in 1260. Sources say that the military orders' native levies betrayed the Crusaders. Whatever happened at Durbe, it was one of the greatest disasters suffered by the Northern Crusaders. The defeat in 1260 led to the "Great Prussian Uprising," in which the Prussians, who had just been subjugated, rose up to wage a war of independence. The conquests of twenty years were undone in a few weeks.

According to some sources, Treniota persuaded his uncle Mindaugas to renounce Christianity. It seemed the first Lithuanian king's conversion had been a political tactic rather than a sincere religious experience. The peace with the Teutonic Order was broken. The Lithuanians attacked the German Crusaders and gave a great deal of support to the rebellious Prussians. The Kingdom of Lithuania was firmly allied with its Baltic kinsmen and women against the Crusaders, who did not recognize it as a sovereign state.

There appears to have been a pagan revival in Lithuania, and it is alleged that Mindaugas publicly sacrificed to the old gods. In truth, outside of the urban centers, paganism was entrenched. However, the Christians, both Catholics and Orthodox Christians, had freedom of religion, and intermarriage was common between the different faiths.

Mindaugas's nephew Treniota became the leader of the Samogitians, demonstrating the close ties between them and the Lithuanian state. He adopted an aggressive approach, even though Mindaugas might have preferred diplomacy or expansion to the east. The first king invaded the Bryansk region to secure the submission of more Slavic princes.

Mindaugas's wife, Morta, was highly influential and was a supporter of the Christianization of Lithuania. Upon her death, Mindaugas married her sister; he might have kidnapped her and forced her to marry him. She was already married to the prince of Pskov. The upset prince allied with Treniota. Mindaugas was assassinated, along with two of his sons, in what is now Latvia. The first and only king of Lithuania had created the first centralized state, but his kingdom became a duchy once more after his death.

Years of Anarchy

Mindaugas's death left a power vacuum in his state and the conquered lands. The chief instigator of the plot to assassinate the king, Treniota, seized power in 1263. Treniota immediately made paganism the state religion, which made him popular with most of the population. He did not make himself a king but ruled as a duke, as he was aware of the unpopularity of monarchs with the Lithuanians. However, Christians and others were not persecuted. He fought wars against the Crusaders and was a great supporter of the Prussians. This included aid during the 1264 siege of Vėluva (Wehlau) castle and reprisals against the Poles for their brutal campaign against the Yotvingians.

Treniota only ruled for a year before he, too, was assassinated by some former servants of the former ruler. One of Mindaugas's sons, Vaišvilkas (also known as Vaišelga), became grand duke after the death of Treniota. He left a monastery to become the ruler in 1264. Interestingly, he did not try to reimpose Christianity as the state religion. He did adopt a policy that was more favorable to the Crusaders, and he halted support for the Prussians and others. This allowed the Teutonic and Livonian Orders to regain some territory and might have contributed to their successful reconquests. Lithuanian territories in Galicia became independent. Vaišvilkas abdicated the Grandy Duchy of Lithuania in 1267 and decided to return to a monastery.

In 1267, Shvarn assumed the title of grand duke despite not being a member of the House of Mindaugas. He was the son-in-law of Mindaugas and ethnically was a Galician. An able warrior and diplomat, he became king of Galicia and seized control of Lithuania in 1267. It does not appear that he had full control of the duchy, and his rule was resisted by many. Despite this, he expanded his territories, defeated the Muslim Volga Tartars, and expanded his rule farther into western Russia. In 1269, he died in what is now Poland; you might have guessed it already, but he was assassinated. Most of his lands came into the possession of Lithuania since he had no legitimate heirs.

By that point, the Grand Duchy of Lithuania was one of the greatest powers in eastern Europe and had vassals in what is now Belarus, Russia, Ukraine, and Poland. It was able to take advantage of the weakness of the Slavic princes by offering them protection. The Mongols of the Golden Horde were not that interested in what happened in this region; they were more interested in tribute than land. As long as the tribute kept flowing, they had little interest in Lithuania's expansion. To the west, Poland suffered from internal divisions. This allowed the fragile duchy to expand despite its chronic instability.

Lithuanian rule respected the rights and traditions of its vassals, unlike the Teutonic Order, and many happily served in its army, as it offered the prospect of booty in raids.

The Beginning of an Empire: Duke Traidenis

After the death of Shvarn, the duchy returned to the House of Mindaugas. Sometime in 1270, the duchy was seized by Traidenis, the powerful duke of Kernavė. Little else is known about him, but he became one of Lithuania's greatest rulers.

Many in Galicia-Volhynia, the stronghold of his predecessor, did not accept his rule. From 1274 to 1276, he fought to control the area, and he was eventually successful. This allowed him to assert more control over his vassals in Ruthenia and Galicia. Traidenis raided deep into Poland. These raids did two things. They enriched the nobility and heavy cavalry upon which the duchy depended, and they ensured that the Poles did not cause mischief in the duchy.

Traidenis ruled Lithuania with a strong hand, and he restored law and order after years of instability after the assassination of the first king of Lithuania. Traidenis was also a gifted diplomat. He married into the Masovian ruling family, who ruled extensive territories in northeastern

Poland, which helped to contain the influence of the Teutonic Order. The duke was a committed pagan and hated the German Crusaders. He established his capital at Kernavė, which was a series of interlinking hill forts and highly defensible. This remarkable site is now a UNESCO World Heritage Site.

In 1270, Traidenis inflicted a massive defeat on the Livonian Order at the Battle of Karuse. The Livonian Order raided Semigallia in modern Latvia, which paid homage to the Grand Duchy of Lithuania. Traidenis gathered a large army and raided the island of Saaremaa (modern Estonia) in response. Grand Master Otto von Lutterberg of the Livonian Order ordered a retreat. The Livonians and the Lithuanians met on the frozen sea near Virtsu. Traidenis knew the German and Danish knights could drive his forces from the field. So, he ordered his men to form barricades with their sleighs on the ice. The Livonian Order attacked the barricades, and they suffered many casualties. Their lines broke when the Lithuanians and their allies counterattacked. Grand Master von Lutterberg died.

In 1272, the Livonian Order established a castle on Lithuanian lands and was able to resist a siege by Traidenis. In 1279, the Livonians invaded Lithuanian territory again with a large army. At the time, the duchy was suffering from a famine and could not offer any effective resistance. This allowed the Livonians to press deep into the duchy, capturing slaves and much booty. The Crusaders became overconfident, and the grand master sent some of his men to their homes with their loot. Seeing this, the Lithuanians launched a surprise attack at Aizkraukle. During it, they killed the grand master. The Battle of Aizkraukle was a disaster for the Livonians, and they lost any autonomy they had. In the future, the grand master of the Teutonic Order was also the master of the Livonian Order.

Traidenis died in his bed in 1282, a remarkable feat for any medieval ruler. He left behind an extensive state.

To conclude, the 13th century witnessed the growth of the first Lithuanian state, which briefly followed the European pattern and became a Christian kingdom. It did not remain one, which changed the trajectory of Lithuania's history. The pressure of the Northern Crusades resulted in the emergence of a state based on war, and this quickly established an empire in what is now Lithuania, Russia, Belarus, and Ukraine.

Chapter Three – Life and Death Struggles with the Crusaders

Endless Wars with the Crusaders

Until the 1280s, the Lithuanians had been spared the brunt of the Northern Crusades. This was to change in the 1280s. In 1284, the Teutonic Order finally crushed the Prussians after a genocidal campaign. The remaining pagan and free Prussians sought sanctuary in Lithuania. From then on, the Teutonic Order and its sister order, the Livonians, could concentrate on the Lithuanians. They became fixated on the narrow corridor of land that connected the duchy to the Baltic Sea because it divided the lands of the Crusading orders in two.

However, this was the territory of the fierce semi-independent Lithuanian tribe, the Samogitians, who were the most steadfast in their paganism. Lithuania was well prepared for the onslaught, as it was prosperous and could draw on a seasoned army of heavy cavalry and infantry. Additionally, its core lands were dotted with hill forts in rough terrain.

The Rise of the House of Gediminas

Daumantas was possibly a relative of Mindaugas, but this is not clear. He became the ruler of the duchy upon the death of Traidenis in 1282. He invaded the Russian principality of Tver in 1285, and he was killed in a battle of which little is known. This led to a succession crisis, as Daumantas had no legitimate sons. He was succeeded by Butigeidis, a relative, or he was selected by the powerful nobility whose armed retinues formed the basis of the army, especially its cavalry. We know little about the new duke, but he was alarmed at the Teutonic Order's successes, and he launched a raid on Prussia in 1284. The new duke responded to the construction of a Crusader castle on the Neman River by building several fortifications to defend his lands.

Butigeidis began a strategy of building fortresses to protect the Lithuanians and their allies, and this was continued by his successors. These fortifications were a departure from the traditional hill forts, and many are stone castles like what the Teutonic Order built. The duke also signed a peace treaty with Galicia in return for a strategic market town, which allowed him to concentrate on the growing threat of the Crusader orders from both the west and the north.

Butigeidis died suddenly, possibly of natural causes. He is regarded as the first member of the House of Gediminas who played a decisive role in Eastern European history. After he died in 1290 or 1291, he was succeeded by his brother, Butvydas, who had been his co-ruler. This pattern of succession would become common in Lithuanian history. Little is known of his reign, but he continued his predecessor's policy of building castles. He also regularly fought the Teutonic Knights and their Livonian allies. Every winter, when the ground was hard enough, as much of Lithuania was marshy, the German Crusaders launched raids. The knights were accompanied by crossbowmen and local levies from among the conquered Baltic populations. During these raids, villages were burned, and people were enslaved. The Lithuanians attacked Prussian lands in retaliation. There were few pitched battles; it was more of a war of skirmishes, ambushes, and raids. Butvydas died in 1295. It is not known how he died.

The Reign of Vytenis

Vytenis was born in 1260, and he was the son of Butvydas and the nephew of Butigeidis. The first mention of him in the written accounts is about his role in the first attack on the Polish state of Masovia. The new duke, who was crowned in 1295, was a strategist, and he became involved in Polish affairs. Traditionally, the Lithuanians had a close relationship with Masovia, which sought a decentralized and fractious Poland, as they feared that a strong Polish state could be a threat. Vytenis supported the duke of Masovia, who had married into the Lithuanian nobility, which ensured that his territories did not become part of a centralized Polish state. He continued his predecessors' policy of building fortresses, and he began to build strongholds on the Jūra River.

By the 1290s, the Teutonic Order had recovered its strength, and it launched yearly raids into Samogitia, which had become all but part of the duchy by this date. Vytenis gave command of the area to a Lithuanian noble who was not a local. He was charged with defending the area, but he also sought to undermine the local Samogitian nobility.

Vytenis was defending Samogitia, but at the same time, he was strengthening his hold over the area. Many Samogitian nobles joined the Teutonic Order, but most accepted the fact that Vytenis's authority was growing. They hated the Christian invaders who wanted to destroy their way of life. The Livonian Order regularly launched raids from the north, and they slowly but surely reconquered lands lost after the Battle of Aizkraukle. By 1313, they had succeeded in regaining what they had lost.

While Vytenis was on the defensive against the Crusaders, he was able to go on the attack to the south. He reconquered many of the lands that had been lost after the death of Mindaugas, including the important Principality of Pinsk (part of modern Russia). In the early 1300s, he went on the offensive against the Teutonic Order and regularly raided their lands. In 1308, Vytenis sacked the town of Brodnica, slaughtering many innocent people. The conflict between the Lithuanians and German Crusaders was brutal, even by medieval standards.

Wars of Conquest

Vytenis took advantage of the division in the Livonian lands. Riga was ruled by its bishops, and he and the citizens began to resent the fiscal demands of the Crusader order. The Rigans allied with the Lithuanians, who garrisoned their city until 1313. While they eventually had to leave, their occupation of Riga boosted trade, and many German merchants began to trade in Lithuanian territories.

The duke was very aware of the importance of religion in his multi-ethnic state. He was instrumental in establishing the Metropolitanate of Lithuania to administer his many Orthodox Christian subjects and allowed Catholic friars to establish religious houses, making him popular with the growing Catholic population, mostly Poles, in the towns. By this time, most of the duchy's population was Orthodox Christians, while the military elite remained mostly pagan.

Little is known about the death of the able ruler, but he was another victim of the assassin's blade in 1316. Nevertheless, he left Lithuania in a strong position and did much to build the state and turn it into an empire.

After the death of Vytenis, his brother or cousin Gediminas succeeded him. Scholars consider him to be the first ruler to hold the title of grand duke of Lithuania. His predecessors had only called themselves dukes, apart from Mindaugas, who had called himself king. Despite the successes of his predecessor, the raids and attacks of the military orders continued. Large tracts of land in Samogitia and Semigallia had become wastelands. Moreover, while the new territories were vast, they were underpopulated.

Gediminas took a potential risk by opening negotiations with the papacy, which had immense prestige in Europe. He exchanged letters with the pope and dangled the prospect of conversion to Catholicism. He also even offered to open up his lands to German and other western European immigrants, which was already happening.

Gediminas was partly motivated by the growing power of the Teutonic Order in Poland. It had recently seized lands in Pomerania, and this had forced the grand duke to raid these lands. Succeeding dukes used their paganism and the prospect of converting to secure diplomatic gains from both the Catholics in the west and the Orthodox Christians in the east. The Lithuanian dukes played the Catholics and Orthodox Christians off each other to win concessions, but they remained steadfast in their loyalty to the old faith.

However, as the Lithuanians conquered more lands populated by the Orthodox Christians, they faced a dilemma. To ensure the obedience and loyalty of the local Slavs, they often intermarried with members of the local families, and this required many pagan nobles to be baptized. Many of them became Christians because of these intermarriages. While the dukes could tolerate Christians, they knew that key supporters, like the nobles and the Samogitians, would turn on them if they were seen as becoming too close to the hated enemy. While the successors of Mindaugas, including Gediminas, dangled the prospect of conversion to their Christian neighbors, they could not fully convert because of the popular support for the old polytheistic faith.

Power of the Pagans

The Lithuanian duke's policy toward the papacy and his promise of conversion made him unpopular with his pagan relatives and his Orthodox subjects, who disliked the idea of being ruled by a Catholic ruler. The duke ended contact with the pope, leading to more Crusader raiding. Catholic clergy operating in Gediminas's lands suffered periodic persecution, and two were executed.

Gediminas expanded Lithuanian lands farther than his predecessors. The Ruthenian and Kievan Rus' princes had never recovered from the Mongol invasions. The major power in the area was the Mongolian Empire, known as the Golden Horde. Its capital was located on the distant Volga in southern Russia. The Duchy of Lithuania was able to avoid outright war despite expanding into the lands of the Mongolian vassal states because once the Golden Horde received their taxes, they were content.

Gediminas signed a peace treaty with the Teutonic Order and the emerging Principality of Muscovy. He then advanced into what is modern Ukraine. At first, Gediminas attacked the Ruthenian Kingdom of Galicia (modern Poland), which had previously been his ally. At an unknown site, the Lithuanians defeated the Ruthenians and killed their king. Gediminas, seeking more glory, proceeded to invade the territory of distant Kiev. Before the Mongol invasions in the 13th century, it had been the most important Rus' state. Sometime in the early 1320s, the Lithuanians advanced to the Irpin River, some thirty kilometers from Kiev. They faced a coalition of local kings and nobles, but the Lithuanians surprised and routed them, killing two local kings and many nobles. In one account, the duke installed a viceroy in Ukraine. However, our sources from the period are scant, and some historians believe the Lithuanians exaggerated their claims.

The growing power of the Baltic duchy aroused the ire of the Mongols. Twice in the 1330s, the Golden Horde attacked Smolensk, but the Lithuanians repelled them after hard fighting. The army of the Grand Duchy of Lithuania was more than the equal of the Mongols, who are often regarded as some of the fiercest warriors in history.

In 1336, the Lithuanians fended off a huge Teutonic Knight invasion, although they had many foreign volunteers. Crusading was a religious duty for many European knights, and many joined this raid, including King John of Bohemia, the famous blind warrior monarch who died at the Battle of Crécy in 1346.

Gediminas was a capable administrator, and he established a nascent government structure that was not based on the loyalty of local elites. He was interested in economic development and is credited with the foundation of Vilnius after he dreamed of an iron wolf. A pagan priest interpreted the dream as meaning he would have to find a city. Sometime in the 1320s, he made Vilnius his capital; it is still the capital of Lithuania today.

A tolerant ruler, Gediminas protected Muslims, Christians, and Jews, but he remained a pagan. The circumstances around his death are obscure, but he was mostly likely the victim of a political assassination. Gediminas founded the dynasty named after him, and he created a true Lithuanian state. Today, he is revered as a national hero. By the time of his death, his realm encompassed modern Lithuania, much of Belarus, part of Poland, Russia, and much of Ukraine.

Pagan Lithuania

There is little information on the social history of pagan Lithuania, but the burial of Gediminas offers us some insights. His funeral was attended by a semi-legendary pagan chief priest. The dead ruler was cremated, and at his funeral, several of his slaves were sacrificed, their corpses thrown on the funeral pyre. The monarch's remains were interred with several of his horses. From the description of the burial, we can see that the Lithuanian elite remained committed pagans. Interestingly, the slaves killed included Germans, who were probably abducted during a raid. The impact of widespread slavery on Lithuanian society made the nobility richer, which came at the expense of the free Lithuanian peasants.

Gediminas was succeeded by his son Jaunutis in 1341, who had an uneventful reign. Jewina or Jaunė, the queen mother, had a profound influence at this time, and she was the power behind the throne. This might have contributed to the coup that led to the deposition of Jaunutis, who was allowed to retire after being forced to abdicate. He was succeeded by his brother Algirdas (r. 1345-1377). Upon the death of Gediminas, his sons became rulers of various regions under Grand Duke Algirdas. The duchy was very much a family business. Algirdas's brother, Kęstutis, was left in control of the western lands and was effectively the co-ruler with his brother. The two siblings worked together very well, and Algirdas could concentrate on the eastern lands where he fought many battles in Ukraine since the power of the Mongols was waning.

Algirdas was able to secure his lands by dynastic alliances or by placing relatives in positions of power. His son, for example, was made prince of Pskov. While the Lithuanian dukes ruled extensive lands, their grip on them was often tenuous and depended as much on diplomacy and marriage alliances as it did on arms.

The duke sought to push to the Black Sea. In 1359, the khan of the Golden Horde died, and his empire was divided into several factions. One ulus or group established a state in Crimea and raided Kiev, which they claimed. The Lithuanians and Mongols met each other at an unknown site; this battle is now known as the Battle of the Blue Waters, and it took place in either 1362 or 1363. According to later sources, the Lithuanians formed into six units and came under attack from the famed horse archers of the Mongols and their allies. Algirdas's units were attacked from a distance by the horse archers, but their armor and shields protected them. Despite the constant arrows from the Mongols and their allies, the Eastern Slavs pressed on and used their heavy cavalry to break the Mongol lines. The duchy's army achieved a total victory.

Relations with the Principality of Muscovy, the strongest of the Russian princedoms, deteriorated over the control of the great trading Republic of Novgorod. Algirdas initiated the First Muscovy-Lithuanian War (1368-1372), during which he raided Moscow and besieged it briefly. At this time, Lithuania was the most powerful state in eastern Europe.

Algirdas controlled, at least on paper, lands from the Baltic to the Black Sea. The duke was able to control a lot of territory because he could count on his brother to defend his lands against the Teutonic Order. He was fairly tolerant like his predecessors and even took an interest in the Metropolitanate of Lithuania. However, he executed Catholic missionaries who defied his orders.

Algirdas married Princess Maria of Vitebsk, a member of the Greek Orthodox faith. However, he prohibited proselytizing. When three of Maria's entourage began to preach in public, they were cruelly executed in 1347. Later, they were canonized by the Orthodox Church and are revered as Saints Anthony, John, and Eustathius, collectively known as the martyrs of Vilnius. In general, Christians enjoyed freedom of religion, but they had to be cautious.

Algirdas was popular with the pagan nobility. He was a pagan, and upon his death, he was given a traditional pagan funeral and buried with eighteen horses. Algirdas was the last truly pagan grand duke, and he expanded the lands of Lithuania to their greatest extent. During this time, the Lithuanian state began to use a style of government based on Ruthenian models, and tribal identities became less pronounced. The various tribes referred to themselves more and more as Lithuanian.

Rise of Moscow

It seemed that at the time of Algirdas's death, the last pagan state in Europe was flourishing. In reality, it was in a weakened state. The Duchy of Moscow was rising, and the German military orders and colonists continued to prove a threat. Moreover, Lithuanian society was changed because of the growing practice of slavery. It was becoming a semi-feudal society, and despite being avowedly pagan, the majority of its two million inhabitants were Orthodox Christians or Catholics. Most of the boyars or nobles were landowners who often owned slaves and who served as heavy cavalry in the duchy's army. The strategic and religious questions facing Lithuanians were eventually resolved by a historic royal marriage.

Chapter Four – From Paganism to Christianity and from Duchy to Commonwealth

The Duke's Opportunity

The conqueror of the Mongols was succeeded by his son Jogaila in 1377. It appears that upon his accession to the throne, he ruled with his uncle, Kęstutis, Duke of Trakai, who ruled the western lands. Jogaila ruled the eastern lands and the huge Ruthenian territories.

Soon, the dual system of government, which had worked so well under his father, broke down. The rise of Moscow prompted the grand duke to become allies with the Mongols. Jogaila could not come to the aid of his new allies, the Golden Horde, at the Battle of Kulikovo in 1380. At this battle, Muscovy defeated the Mongols, which marked the duchy's rapid rise to power. Later, the Lithuanians took advantage of the Mongols' weakness and invaded their lands. If Jogaila knew how much the Lithuanians would suffer at the hands of the successors of Muscovy, the Russian tsars, he would have done everything possible to join his Mongolian allies in the battle.

Jogaila grew suspicious of his uncle, and he formed a secret treaty with an enemy, the Teutonic Knights. This started the First Lithuanian Civil War. Kęstutis and his son Vytautas were enraged by this agreement with the hated Crusaders and seized Vilnius, the capital. A weakened Jogaila appeared to offer negotiations, but he tricked his uncle and cousin and imprisoned them. Kęstutis was later found murdered, and Vytautas was forced to flee from the Teutonic Knights.

In 1382, Jogaila signed the Treaty of Dubysa, and he committed to the Christianization of his lands. The Lithuanian duke reneged on the treaty, possibly because of pagan opposition. This prompted the Teutonic Order to raid his lands in 1383 with his cousin Vytautas, who had become a Christian. Jogaila changed tactics and invited Vytautas to regain his dukedom. Together, they began to raid Prussia.

The geopolitical situation was changing. To the east of Lithuania was the Duchy of Moscow, which was growing stronger by the year despite being officially a Mongol vassal, and to the west and north lay the Christian military orders.

Jogaila was unmarried, and he was expected to enter a political marriage to further his dynasty's interests. His mother was from Muscovy, and she wanted him to marry an Orthodox Christian. It seems likely that he would have married one but for a remarkable proposal.

A Historic Marriage

In the 1380s, Poland underwent a succession crisis. It had been in a personal union with Hungary under Louis the Great, a member of the French Angevin House. After his early death, his two daughters stood to inherit either Hungary or Poland. Louis's younger daughter Jadwiga was duly crowned monarch in Krakow in 1384, even though she was only a child.

Poland's nobility wanted a strong ruler, one who could protect their interests against the growing power of the Teutonic Knights. This prompted some of them to do something remarkable. With the permission of eleven-year-old Jadwiga and her mother, a marriage proposal was offered to Jogaila despite the age difference and the fact the young queen was Catholic and the Lithuanian duke a pagan.

This was a geopolitical bombshell. Jogaila readily agreed, as he would become the king of Poland and ruler of Lithuania, making him one of the most powerful rulers in all of Europe. Lithuania would also benefit because it would have a powerful ally against its historic enemies, the Teutonic Knights and Muscovy. Moreover, many of the nobility had become Orthodox Christians, and the core territories of Lithuania were slowly becoming Christianized. The duke guessed that the conversion of Lithuania was inevitable.

The terms of the marriage are outlined in what is known as the Union of Krewo (1385). The most important term was that Jogaila had to convert to Catholicism and obey the authority of the pope in Rome. It also attached all the Lithuanian lands to the Polish realm. In effect, the union was a personal one, and Jogaila would become king of Poland and the ruler of Lithuania.

In 1386, Jagiello traveled to the Polish capital of Krakow and married Jadwiga. He was crowned king of Poland, which is seen as the beginning of the new Jagiellon dynasty. This led to the majority of the Lithuanian court and the nobility becoming Catholics and shunning paganism. In the spring of 1388, the townspeople and peasants, under pressure from the nobility, received baptism in the rivers of the duchy. The Catholic Church quickly moved into Lithuania. It established a cathedral in Vilnius in 1387 and introduced a parish system in the core lands. Pagan temples were torn down and often replaced by parish churches. Any vestiges of paganism became targeted for destruction. Thus ended the last pagan state of Europe.

Or did it? The countryside remained pagan, and there was no mass persecution of the old pagan priests. Many household cults continued. While many people in the rural areas went to Catholic Mass, they remained pagan. The disputed territory of the Samogitians was also pagan since it was technically not part of Lithuania at this time, as it had been ceded to the Teutonic Order. Here, the old pagan temples still stood, and the house cults of grass snakes still flourished as they had for centuries.

Christianization had dramatic consequences for the Lithuanians. Their state was unified only with Poland because they shared the same ruler. The Lithuanian nobility preserved their liberties and privileges even though they were now Catholics, but they came under growing Polish cultural and political influence. The Catholic Church soon became enormously powerful, and the nobles were able to secure even more privileges and land at the expense of the commoners.

Not everyone accepted the union, and it was not just because of the conversion to Christianity. There was also the perceived submission to Poland that needed to be considered. This led to the Second Lithuanian Civil War (1389-1392). Jogaila, who co-ruled Poland with his queen, was also the grand duke of Lithuania. He had to deal with his cousin Vytautas. He wanted recognition of the rights of Lithuania and his power. Vytautas enlisted the support of the Teutonic Knights against Jogaila. The German knights did not believe that the conversion of Lithuania was sincere, and more importantly, they needed Samogitia to link Prussia with Livonia.

Vytautas and his allies besieged Vilnius, but they could not capture it. Jogaila and his new Polish vassals contained the enemy and forced them to the negotiating table. The new king of Poland conceded the title of grand duke to Vytautas, who would rule in his name. Vytautas was the de facto ruler of Lithuania and its empire. This agreement proved popular in Lithuania.

Vytautas the Grand Duke: Conqueror of the Crusaders

Despite being a subordinate of his cousin Jogaila, Vytautas is regarded as one of the greatest rulers of Lithuania. In 1395, the khan of the Golden Horde was defeated by Timur at the Battle of Terek, which left the Mongols in disarray. Khan Tokhtamysh asked the Lithuanians for help. Vytautas was able to secure more Ruthenian lands, such as Smolensk, and even reached as far as Crimea, where he built a fortress. Because of this expansion, the Duchy of Lithuania became the largest state in all of Europe.

Despite the agreement with Poland, many in Lithuania still resented the growing influence of the Polish nobility, who saw the duchy as an appendage. Infuriated by demands to pay tribute to the Poles, they refused to pay. This led to Vytautas coming to an agreement with the Teutonic Knights for a third time with the Treaty of Salynas in 1398. He agreed to cede the crucial area of Samogitia to the Crusaders. However, the Samogitians resented their incorporation into Prussia. Vytautas needed peace to resist the Poles, though. The Teutonic Order benefited from this arrangement, and they could finally link their lands to that of their Livonian brethren.

Vytautas wanted to conquer all the Ruthenian lands, and for this, he needed more assistance. Because Lithuania was a Christian state, it asked the pope to sanction a crusade against the Mongols. Jogaila and Vytautas gathered a huge Christian army and invaded Mongol lands. By this time, the Golden Horde had been able to recover from the defeats inflicted on them by Timur. Vytautas's army met the Mongols at the Vorskla River and fought a massive battle on July 12th, 1399. The khan of the Golden Horde tricked Vytautas with the offer of a temporary truce, but this was a ploy to allow for more reinforcements to arrive. The battle was a disaster for the Lithuanians, and many members of the elite died. Lithuanian rule ended in the Black Sea region, and the Golden Horde even threatened Kiev. The defeat persuaded the Lithuanians that they needed the assistance of the Poles.

During this time, the Teutonic Order continued to attack Lithuania despite the direct orders of the pope not to do so. The military order needed new lands so it could attract recruits because, as warrior monks, they could not marry and have sons. They simply had to continue to attack the Lithuanians even if they had become, at least on paper, Catholics.

Vytautas was able to form a new army and soon regained many Ruthenian lands. The Lithuanians agreed on a favorable peace treaty with the Duchy of Moscow after a standoff at the Urga River, where the Muscovites had established a line of forts. This divided what is now northwestern Russia between the rivals.

19th-century painting of the Battle of Grunwald by Jan Matejko.[3]

The Battle of Grunwald: The Largest Battle of the Middle Ages

Vytautas could now concentrate on the Crusaders. In 1409, he incited the Samogitians to revolt. The Teutonic Order invaded Poland, which played into the hands of the Lithuanians, as they could now be guaranteed the support of the Poles against the Germans. After a brief truce, fighting resumed in December 1409. In June 1410, the Polish-Lithuanian army, reinforced by its vassals and mercenaries, invaded Prussia, taking the Teutonic Order by surprise. The army was led by Vytautas, and he built a pontoon bridge to allow his vast army to cross the Vistula undetected.

However, Grand Master Ulrich von Jungingen was able to assemble a large army. He was confident, which makes sense; he had some of the finest knights in Europe. The grand master had intended to defeat Poland and Lithuanians separately, but he had been outwitted by Vytautas. Vytautas and King Władysław II (Jogaila) agreed to join forces and march on the Teutonic Order's headquarters at Marburg Castle. Jogaila, as the king of Poland, was in overall command, but Vytautas was the commander. The armies were both huge for the time, and they included heavy cavalry units of knights, crossbowmen, infantry, and even early forms of cannons known as bombards.

On July 15th, the two huge armies gathered at the village of Grunwald, which today is in northern Poland. The exact number of the forces is unknown, but the subsequent Battle of Grunwald is often cited as the largest battle in medieval European history. The Lithuanian forces and cavalry massed on the left, the mercenaries and allies were stationed in the center, and the Poles were on the right.

Vytautas charged the Prussian right. Some historians reported that he ordered a feigned retreat, which he learned from fighting the Mongols of the Golden Horde. The Teutonic Knights attacked the Poles, and they were hard-pressed; at one point, King Władysław was almost surrounded by the Germans. Then, the Lithuanians under Vytautas returned to the battlefield and attacked the Germans in the rear. They were caught by complete surprise, and the knights tried to build a wagon fort to defend themselves, but this failed. The Lithuanians killed many knights, and their allies and vassals fled.

The Battle of Grunwald was a disaster for the German Crusader order. One source claims that only a fraction of the Teutonic Knights and soldiers returned to Marienburg Fortress. Much of the German order's leadership was captured and beheaded on the orders of Vytautas, including the grand master.

The Polish-Lithuanian army marched on Marburg, but its defenders were able to resist under the command of the new grand master, Heinrich von Plauen. Vytautas besieged Marienburg Fortress in Marburg from July until September, but he had not prepared for a long siege, and his army desired to return home for the harvest. The Peace of Thorn was signed between both sides. The terms were not that unfavorable to the German Crusaders, and it was not able to secure a lasting peace. In 1414, the so-called Hunger War broke out when the Germans and the Polish-Lithuanians adopted scorched earth tactics, causing a famine.

The victory at Grunwald had shown the Poles that the Lithuanians could be crucial and would help them protect their eastern flank against enemies like the Principality of Muscovy. Both the grand duke of Lithuania and the king of Poland signed the Union of Vilnius in 1413. Under this treaty, Lithuania became part of Poland as an equal partner. Both states had to choose their leader, the grand duke in the case of Lithuania, and both sides had to agree on the other's choice of leader. The new union was to continue after the death of the existing grand duke and king. It also stipulated that the Polish and Lithuanian nobility had the same rights. The nobles formed into a single college, beginning the Polonization of the Lithuanian elite.

Vytautas ruled a religiously diverse set of territories, and he practiced religious tolerance. At one point, he tried to reconcile the Orthodox and the Catholic Churches. Samogitian was the last bastion of paganism, but even here, according to the archaeological record, pagan burials had begun to decline by the late 14th century. In 1413, the Samogitians formally accepted Christianity, but it seems only half-heartedly.

After the victory at Grunwald, Vytautas was the most powerful ruler in eastern Europe. By this time, the Golden Horde had all but collapsed and was replaced by smaller khanates. Vytautas was able to make many Tartars, as the Mongols had become known, his vassals. The Principality of Muscovy also came under his influence.

In 1422, war broke out between the Teutonic Order and the Poles and Lithuanians again. Vytautas attacked Prussia while the order was distracted by the raids of the heretic Hussites. The Poles and Lithuanians seized land and fortresses, and the Germans quickly agreed to the Treaty of Menlo. The Teutonic Order ceded lands to Lithuania, and this was to be the border between Prussia and the Duchy of Lithuania for the next half a millennium.

In 1429, an assembly of Lithuanian nobles urged Vytautas to become king of Lithuania, which sparked a crisis with Poland. However, the grand duke refused to accept the crown. This indicates that Lithuania, despite its vast empire, which covered much of present-day Belarus, Ukraine, and western Russia, needed Poland, and this ensured that the union between the two states continued despite the tensions. The union provided a measure of stability, and it secured the allegiance of both Catholic and Orthodox Christian elites.

In 1430, Vytautas died, and his death ended the Golden Age of Lithuania. The following years would be marked by instability, decline, and the growing influence of Poland over Lithuanian lands.

The Jews of Lithuania

Despite the Duchy of Lithuania being a pagan political entity, it was not an intolerant society. Christians, both Catholic and Orthodox, and others who showed loyalty were tolerated. There is evidence that Lithuanian Christians and immigrants could practice their faith freely from an early date.

Jews are believed to have settled in Lithuania at an early date. Many of these refugees came because of religious persecution in their homeland. There is the possibility that these early Jews came to the duchy from Khazaria after its destruction by the Rus' in the 10th century CE. Khazaria was a Turkic empire whose elite had converted to Judaism.

Lithuanian rulers appreciated skilled immigrants and traders since they could boost the economy, which was needed to sustain the army. This pragmatic approach can be seen in the letter of Gediminas dated to the 14th century. He invited German merchants and craftspeople to settle in his realm. To incentivize them, they were accorded special privileges and could even form guilds. Historians believe that among these early German settlers were Jews.

In 1388, the union of Lithuania and Poland resulted in the official Christianization of Lithuania. This encouraged Christian merchants and others to live in Lithuanian towns and its capital, Vilnius. In 1388, a charter was issued for Trakai, an important town, that granted legal privileges to Jews. They had the status of freemen, and in court cases, they had the status of a member of the lower nobility. These rights for Jews were most unusual at the time, and they attracted Jewish immigrants and others who greatly contributed to the Lithuanian economy. Poland had been tolerant of Jews, and this, no doubt, persuaded the Lithuanian dukes to grant this ethnoreligious group a special status. Jews could only be brought before courts presided over by special representatives of the duke.

After the union of Poland and Lithuania, the Jews prospered. This changed in 1495 when Grand Duke Alexander of Lithuania expelled the Jews, possibly so that he would not have to pay his father's debts to Jewish merchants. When Alexander became king of Poland, he rescinded his order, and the exiles were permitted to return home. The Jews were too useful to the king.

The Jewish community was large, and they mainly lived in urban centers. However, restrictions were gradually placed on their residency in Vilnius in the 16th century. Most were involved in trade, but more affluent Jews worked for the government as tax collectors. This might have resulted in growing anti-Semitism among the peasantry. Karaite Jews also settled in Lithuania; they were Turkic-speaking Jews who differed in their practices and beliefs from Rabbinic Jews. Few Karaite communities exist today. A tiny one can still be found in Lithuania. This diversity ultimately strengthened the Lithuanian state and allowed it to become a great power.

By the 15th century, Lithuania was home to a thriving Jewish community at a time when they suffered oppression and persecution in the rest of Europe. This is a testament to the power of the Grand Duchy of Lithuania, as tolerance is a characteristic of solid states and societies.

Chapter Five – Wars with Russia and the Union of Lublin (1430–1570)

After Vytautas, who had no male heir, died, there was a power vacuum. This was inevitable; the grand duke had been such a towering figure. This led to the Third Lithuanian Civil War (1432-1438). One of the claimants to the duchy, Švitrigaila, a son of Algirdas, revolted and entered an alliance with the Teutonic Order, which threatened to break up the union. The Poles backed Sigismund Kęstutaitis, the son of former Grand Duke Kęstutis and the brother of Vytautas. With the support of the Poles, he became grand duke in 1432, but he only became the effective ruler when he was able to decisively defeat the Švitrigaila faction and the Teutonic Knights at the Battle of Wiłkomierz in 1435.

Sigismund Kęstutaitis only ruled for eight years before he was murdered in 1440. There was again the threat of another civil war. The Lithuanian nobility was concerned by this because it came at a time when the Duchy of Muscovy was becoming more assertive. Casimir (1427-1492), the son of Jogaila, was elected unilaterally by the Lithuanian nobility as the grand duke. While this guaranteed stability, it also led to a break in the Union of Krewo. However, the Poles were pragmatic and accepted the new grand duke.

In 1446, Casimir was elected as Casimir IV of Poland after the death of his brother Władysław III of Poland, who died during the Battle of Varna in 1444 when the Ottoman Turks crushed a Crusader army. Casimir remained the grand duke of Lithuania. A faction of Polish nobles sought to prevent his coronation, but the majority wanted him to become their monarch to ensure stability.

Casimir was a successful ruler and can be likened in his centralizing and progressive policies to monarchs like Henry VII of England and Louis XI of France. Under Casimir's careful rule, the economies of both Lithuania and Poland improved.

In 1454, the Prussian cities rose in revolt against the Teutonic Knights, and Casimir intervened on behalf of the rebels. This led to the Thirteen Years' War (1454-1466), which weakened the Teutonic Order and was a great victory for Casimir and particularly the Poles. Prussia became a vassal of Poland. Poland also recovered Pomerania. This meant that the western borders of Lithuania were secured, which was essential since the situation in the east was getting worse for the Grand Duchy of Lithuania. This was because of the continued rise of the dukes of Moscow and the emergence of a new power, the Ottoman Turks, who proved to be as formidable as the former Golden Horde.

Wars with the Russians

By the 15th century, power in the Lithuanian lands lay in the hands of a series of magnates, and these families held immense military, economic, and political power. Like elsewhere in eastern Europe, feudalism became more common. The peasantry had to pay their lord's rent and perform other obligations, including military service. Society became less equal and more hierarchal. Traditionally, Lithuanians had been equal, but this was lost as the tribal organization of society gave way to one based on feudalism. The rights of the peasantry were less than those in medieval western Europe, and they were gradually reduced to the status of a serf, a form of bondage likened to slavery. Lithuanians were only a minority in the lands they ruled, and they needed the cooperation of local Orthodox elites to rule their lands and serve in their army.

Under Casimir IV, Lithuania enjoyed peace for much of the 15th century. Its lands extended to within one hundred miles of Moscow and south to Kyiv, and its influence reached the shores of the Black Sea.

The Crimean Khanate had been subjugated by Vytautas the Great, but they had been able to achieve almost total independence after his death. Lithuania was able to contain the Crimean Tartars and prevented their slave raids.

In 1453, the Ottoman Turks captured Constantinople after a siege. Originally nomads fleeing the Mongols, they had become the most powerful state in the eastern Mediterranean and the Middle East. The Crimean Tartars became their vassals, and with Ottoman support, they went on the offensive. They launched long-distance raids on the steppes and raided as far as what is now Belarus. During these raids, they caused havoc and captured and enslaved those they did not kill. In 1487, they managed to sack Kyiv and placed thousands of its citizens into slavery.

These raids indirectly led to the rise of the Cossacks, who were initially individuals fleeing serfdom who ventured into the no-man's land created by the Crimean depredations. They defended the area in the south against the Muslim Tartars and launched counterraids. The Lithuanian dukes came to recognize the Cossacks and might have appointed their leader or hetman, which is believed to come from a Lithuanian word. Cossacks came to form semi-autonomous settlements in what is now Ukraine.

Nevertheless, the Lithuanians began to lose influence over its southernmost lands. Casimir IV, King of Poland and Grand Duke of Lithuania, died in 1492 and was succeeded by his son, John I Albert Jagiellon, as king of Poland and by his brother, Alexander, as grand duke of Lithuania.

The Rise of Moscow

The power of Muscovy had long worried Lithuania and Poland. Under Prince Ivan III, known as Ivan the Great, its power increased significantly. First, he was able to secure independence from what was left of the Golden Horde in 1480. He later conquered or subdued the core Russian lands. Ivan III was a shrewd ruler and built a strong state that was populous and rich in resources.

The Grand Duchy of Lithuania's rule over its many provinces was not very firm, especially after the death of Vytautas. Ivan III and his successors began to compete with the duchy for control of these areas. Moscow believed it was the heir of Kievan Rus', and it wanted to rule all the Eastern Slavs who belonged to the Orthodox faith.

It soon became clear that Lithuania needed the support of the Poles if they were to keep their lands in what is now Russia, Ukraine, and Belarus. In 1487, the Muscovites began to attack along its frontier with Lithuania, and they allied with the Tartars. In 1492, Ivan launched a full-scale invasion of the duchy. Many Orthodox nobles welcomed the Muscovites, as they had begun to resent Catholic rule.

The war ended with the marriage of the grand duke, Alexander, to a Muscovite princess. However, in 1500, Ivan III broke the treaty, as the Poles had declared war on the Ottoman Empire and could not assist the duchy. Without the Poles, the Lithuanians were vulnerable. A large Muscovite army marched into Lithuanian territory, and in response, the Lithuanians assembled a large army.

The two forces met at the Vedrosha River, some one hundred kilometers south of Moscow. The sources for this battle are scarce, but the Muscovites used tactics that had proven successful against the Tartars of the Golden Horde. The Russians waited until they and the Lithuanians were engaged in fierce close-quarters combat. They then launched a surprise attack by sending a concealed cavalry unit into the rear of the Lithuanians, whose allies broke and fled. This battle was a disaster for the duchy, as it lost thousands of seasoned veterans. In the words of one historian, in one day, the Lithuanians lost what had taken them two centuries to attain in the east. The highest-ranking military officer, the hetman, was also captured.

Alexander Jagiellon became the ruler of the Polish-Lithuanian state in 1501 after his brother, King John I Albert of Poland, died. He decided to adopt a more diplomatic approach, given the huge losses that the Lithuanians had suffered. He proposed a union between the Orthodox and the Catholic Churches. Although this failed, it bought the duchy some time. Moscow continued to make progress, and by the time the war had ended, it had captured around one-third of the Lithuanian empire.

Alexander was not well liked in Poland, as he was thought to have favored his fellow Balts. Moreover, he was continually short of funds. The Polish nobles in the Sejm or Parliament forced him to agree to allow the council to veto his orders related to the aristocracy. This was a crucial step in the creation of a noble democracy, as it meant that an assembly of nobles could vote on state policy. As a result, Alexander had more power as a grand duke in Lithuania than as a king in Poland.

Alexander's favorite was a Lithuanian nobleman of Tartar descent named Michael Glinski, who was hated by the Poles in particular. In 1506, he was made a marshal and led an army against raiding Tartars, defeating them in the Battle of Kleck. According to some sources, he poisoned King Alexander. Glinski rebelled after Alexander's death, as he was stripped of his powers, and allied with Muscovy under the banner of defending the Orthodox Church. The conflict took place between 1507 and 1508. The Lithuanians and Poles crushed the rebellion, and there was a peace agreement with Moscow.

Another war broke out in 1512. Moscow seized the strategic city of Smolensk. However, King Sigismund the Old (who was also the grand duke of Lithuania) led the Lithuanians better. In 1514, Sigismund the Old led a mostly Polish army against the Russians at Orsha. Muscovy had a much larger army, but their commander was overconfident. An attack on the Polish-Lithuanian flank failed, which weakened their center. This allowed the Polish Winged Hussars (heavy cavalry) to attack the center and rout the Russian army, inflicting significant losses. The victory at Orsha gave Lithuania a stable eastern frontier for several decades.

Painting of the Battle of Orsha, attributed to Hans Krell.[4]

The Lithuanian Reformation and Counter-Reformation

The Protestant Reformation led to a schism in Christianity between Catholics and Protestants, unleashing centuries of religious unrest and war in Europe. The Polish-Lithuanian dependency of Prussia became a hotbed of Protestantism, specifically Lutheranism. Lithuanian intellectuals came under the influence of Lutheranism but suffered persecution for their beliefs.

In Poland, many magnates came to support Protestantism, which made it more popular in Lithuania. By the 1550s, there was a reformed church based on the principles of Calvinism. By this time, Lutheranism had a strong presence in Lithuania. It was widely adopted by the sons of the nobility who had studied abroad and by those alienated by a non-Lithuanian-speaking Catholic clergy. Towns like Kaunas adopted Lutheranism. The powerful Radziwiłł family renounced their Catholicism, which was a significant blow to the Catholic Church in Lithuania.

The impact of Protestantism was profound, as it led to a new class of literate scholars who wrote books in Latin. They were interested in preaching to the poor and uneducated, and they began translating the Bible into Lithuanian. The first book to be printed in the Lithuanian language was the *Simple Words of Catechism*, translated by Martynas Mažvydas in 1547. Decades later, Jonas Bretkūnas translated the Bible into Lithuanian. Most of the elite still used Polish. The rural class stayed loyal to Catholicism or at least a faith that was a syncretization of Catholicism and paganism.

The Catholic authorities were alarmed at the advance of Protestantism in the Polish-Lithuanian realm and decided on a reform campaign. At a synod in 1564, they adopted the tenets of the Council of Trent, which sought to revive the Catholic Church and convert those who had embraced the "heresy" of Protestantism. The Catholic Church embarked on a campaign to marginalize the Protestants. In Lithuania, the Catholics published many works on religious controversies and even established a university to counter the dissemination of Protestant ideas. The Jesuit Order was introduced into the Polish-Lithuanian Commonwealth in the 1570s, and the people became active in education and the promotion of Catholic devotional practices.

Sigismund II Augustus (r. 1548–1572), the son of Sigismund the Old, was both a devout Catholic and interested in the new faiths. He exchanged letters with John Calvin, who developed the doctrine of Calvinism. However, he was an ardent Catholic, and many Lithuanian nobles conformed to the monarch's will, which did much to weaken the cause of Protestantism. Two branches of the Radziwiłł family converted back to Catholicism from Calvinism. One branch continued to be Lutherans until the 20th century. The Catholics seized the property of Lutherans and Calvinists and imposed financial levies on them, which coerced many back into the fold of the Catholic Church.

Despite this, the Lutherans and Calvinists were not eradicated, and there are congregations of both faiths to this day. The Orthodox congregations were targeted by Protestant and Catholic missionaries, which led the Greek Orthodox Church to reform its structure and strictly enforce clerical discipline. Catholic clergy, as part of the Counter-Reformation, focused more on the religious practices of the peasantry. Slowly but surely, they relinquished many of the old pagan cults and practices. The Counter-Reformation, in many ways, continued the process of Christianization that had begun in 1386. Nevertheless, some traces of paganism persisted.

The Livonian War

The Livonian War began in 1558 when Ivan IV (1530–1584), better known as Ivan the Terrible, sought to expand Muscovy's influence westward by targeting the weakened Livonian Order. Ivan's ambition to control the Baltic trade routes and access the lucrative ports in the region led to aggressive campaigns. The Livonian Order, which was already struggling with internal instability and external pressures, was ill-prepared to resist Muscovy's initial assaults.

By the early 1560s, the Livonian Order was unable to maintain its defenses. In 1561, the Treaty of Vilnius formally dissolved the Livonian Order, and its territories were divided between Poland-Lithuania and other regional powers. This drew Lithuania and its Polish allies into direct conflict with Ivan IV.

The Polish-Lithuanian Commonwealth's intervention escalated the war into a larger regional conflict, with Ivan IV's forces invading Lithuanian lands and threatening Vilnius. Lithuania's victory at the Battle of Ula in January 1564, led by the Lithuanian hetman Mikołaj Radziwiłł, temporarily halted Russian advances. However, Ivan IV's continued campaigns in Livonia caused widespread devastation and prolonged the conflict.

The Danes and the Swedes entered the war on behalf of Poland and Lithuania. The war continued until 1583, when Livonia was partitioned between Denmark, Sweden, and the Polish-Lithuanian Commonwealth.

The Grand Duchy of Lithuania was able to secure Semigallia, Courland, and much of Livonia.

On the face of it, Lithuania had stabilized its eastern frontier, gained new lands in the Baltic, and was strong, but it had been weakened. Many of the old Orthodox Ruthenian nobles were unhappy, claiming that the duchy had become too dependent on the Catholic Poles.

From Union to Commonwealth

Sigismund the Old had been a successful king of Poland and grand duke of Lithuania. He was widely respected. However, he had no male heir, which led to a crisis for the Jagiellon dynasty and Lithuania. It was also a crisis for the union of Poland and Lithuania, as they had been united through the sovereign. Without a king, the state would dissolve.

The Polish nobles were increasingly powerful in the Sejm (Parliament) and had fought with the Lithuanians against the Russians. By then, the Lithuanian boyars or nobles had become immensely powerful, and they owned vast estates worked by serfs. They were also partly Polonized, using Ruthenian for official purposes, but they still retained their sense of a separate Lithuanian identity.

Sigismund the Old convened a meeting of the Lithuanian and Polish nobility at Lublin to resolve the issue. The Poles had the upper hand, and they pressured the Lithuanians to accept the terms of a political union that was to their advantage. The Lithuanians were obliged to transfer lands to the Poles and to attend the Polish Sejm. The agreement known as the Union of Lublin (1569) was bitterly resented by many in Lithuania, and many nobles threatened to return home. Sigismund was determined and helped to negotiate the agreement that led to the Commonwealth of Poland-Lithuania. The Union of Lublin led to the creation of a single state, replacing the personal union, and it was to be ruled by one monarch with a shared senate and parliament (Sejm). Lithuania lost some of its autonomy and influence, but it had no choice but to agree to the Polish terms because of the Russian threat.

The last of the Jagiellons was Anna (r. 1575–1587), the daughter of Sigismund the Old. A highly educated woman, she was famed for her charitable works. She only married after becoming queen of Poland, and her husband, Stephen Báthory of Hungary, became her consort. Her marriage to him was unhappy, and she sought solace in architectural projects. She was never interested in power, and she abdicated the throne in 1587 and lived quietly in her court. By this time, the Polish and Lithuanian nobility were the de facto rulers of the state.

Anna promoted her niece, also named Anna, as her heir, and she was married to Sigismund Vasa of the Swedish royal house. Her support helped Sigismund to be elected as the king of Poland and the grand duke of Lithuania in 1587. A new era for Lithuanians had begun.

Chapter Six – The Polish-Lithuanian Commonwealth: Rise and Fall (1569–1778)

By the opening years of the 17th century, the Polish-Lithuanian Commonwealth was the most powerful state in eastern Europe. After the Livonian War and the death of Ivan the Terrible in 1584, Russia fell into anarchy and famine. At one point, the Poles and Lithuanians occupied Moscow briefly in 1610.

The Polish-Lithuanian Commonwealth had a unified government, but Lithuania had its own army and legal system. Indeed, even after the Union of Lublin, some Lithuanian nobles believed they still had the right to elect their own grand duke. However, the Lithuanian nobility was increasingly becoming culturally Polish and Catholic. Religious tolerance was the norm in the commonwealth, but it was a majority Catholic state, which caused some friction with religious minorities.

The Grand Duchy of Lithuania was composed of the core Lithuanian lands, Belarus, and some Russian territories, and it co-ruled Livonia with Poland. Its cities were busy and diverse, and the local nobility built magnificent buildings that are still admired today. The king of Poland was always the grand duke, just as he had been in the past. Because the kings of the commonwealth were elected, they had limited powers. Furthermore, many were foreigners and dependent on the local aristocracy. The nobles were the real power in what had become an aristocratic democracy. Under this system, the nobility controlled the Sejm, and any noble could veto the election of a king. The outcome of this over the long term was that the commonwealth's government was weak, and it could not reform.

Conflict with Sweden

In the short term, the Polish-Lithuanian Commonwealth flourished, and it became a leading exporter of grain. The Lithuanian nobility grew immensely rich, and families like the Radziwiłłs became owners of large fiefs and were lavish builders.

Sigismund III Vasa's (r. 1587-1632) election as king is often seen as the beginning of an era of prosperity for Poland and Lithuania. He was Swedish by birth and a committed Catholic, and he wanted to create a centralized state, limiting the power of the aristocracy. Sigismund also briefly became king of Sweden but lost the throne to his uncle because of his intolerance of Protestantism. Sigismund never accepted this, which led to years of enmity with the Swedish. Between 1600 and 1629, a series of Polish-Swedish wars erupted. The conclusion of the Polish-Swedish wars resulted in the Swedes occupying part of Livonia (northern Estonia). Poland-Lithuania did not lose much land and quickly recovered from the wars.

By this point, Russia was engulfed in chaos in the period known as the Time of Troubles. This gave Lithuania years of peace, even though its army was still active on many fronts.

Sigismund III Vasa was also a patron of the arts. Many Western artists and artisans settled in the commonwealth, which was booming economically, as it had the good sense not to become involved in the brutal religious conflict known as the Thirty Years' War. The multi-ethnic and religiously diverse state was peaceful, and its subjects enjoyed religious tolerance and good governance. Vilnius was home to various faiths and became a center of culture and the arts. However, much of the population were serfs and did not benefit from the peace and prosperity.

Sigismund III Vasa's son succeeded him as King Władysław IV of Poland and Grand Duke of Lithuania in 1632. He was a forward-thinking ruler who modernized the army and held the frontiers against the Russians and the Ottoman Turks. However, his successor, John II Casimir, who came to the throne in 1648, was an inept monarch and weak. The Polish-Lithuanian lands had always been ethnically diverse, but some resented the growing influence of Catholicism, especially the

Orthodox Christians. The Polish Catholics provoked a terrible Cossack uprising in Ukraine. These lands had once been ruled by Lithuania, and they were more even-handed and tolerant than the Poles.

Between 1648 and 1668, the commonwealth was wracked by a series of international conflicts known as the Deluge (1648-1666). The Khmelnytsky Uprising (1648-1657), which saw the wholesale massacre of Catholics and Jews, led to the emergence of a Cossack state in Ukraine that was an ally of Russia. Lithuania escaped this disaster. However, it was to suffer in a series of unprecedented disasters that devasted the duchy. It was ill-prepared for a new war with Russia and the Second Northern War with Sweden.

King John II Casimir Vasa (r. 1648-1668) was a devout Catholic who despised non-Catholics. The Lithuanian nobles saw him as a weak king, including the Radziwiłł family, and they allied with Sweden. Under an agreement, the Radziwiłłs would rule the Grand Duchy of Lithuania as a Swedish protectorate. This indicated the growing disillusionment of the Lithuanian elite with the union, as the weakened duchy had come under increasing Polish control. In 1653, Russia declared war on the Polish-Lithuanian Commonwealth. Because of the nobility's strength in Poland, the commonwealth's military was weak, poorly led, and poorly armed. In 1655, the Swedish army of Charles X invaded Polish lands and inflicted a massive defeat on the commonwealth at the Battle of Ujście in July of that year. They then pressed on to Warsaw, as they wanted to depose John II Casimir and install a puppet ruler. Another Swedish army occupied the eastern part of the Grand Duchy of Lithuania, territories in what is now Estonia and Belarus.

Portrait of John II Casimir by Daniel Schultz.[5]

 The Radziwiłłs signed the Union of Kėdainiai in 1655, which terminated the union with Poland. However, this was not accepted in Warsaw. Unlike in previous centuries, the Lithuanians were too weak to protect themselves, and the Russians invaded the core Lithuanian lands, seeking to expand to the Baltic and sensing the weakness of the Radziwiłłs They ravaged the land and committed unspeakable outrages. On August 9th, 1655, they seized Vilnius and massacred much of the population.

 Realizing their weakness, some Lithuanians accepted the grand duchy as a client state of Sweden so that the Swedes could help them against the Russians even though the commonwealth technically was still at war with the Swedes. By the winter of 1655, the Swedes occupied much of Poland, and John II Casimir was in exile. The Russians became so concerned about the growing power of the Swedes that they allied with the Poles. Many, possibly the majority of Lithuanians, opposed the Radziwiłłs and their pro-Swedish policies. They wanted to reestablish the old Polish-Lithuanian Commonwealth, and they fought with the Poles, even though they had become allies of Russia. Polish and some Lithuanian units fought a guerrilla campaign against the Swedes, forcing them back. In the spring of 1656, they almost managed to surround the Swedish army in the forests of Sandomierz.

However, in the open field, the Swedes were invincible and crushed a recently recruited Polish-Lithuanian army at Warsaw in July 1656. The Polish-Lithuanian army freed Lublin and even took part of Warsaw before being defeated at the Battle of Klecko. They were later joined by more Polish forces, and they began to besiege Warsaw with its Swedish garrison. The Polish city fell, and King Charles X of Sweden realized he needed help, so he invited Prussia to join the conflict. Charles wanted to partition Poland between Sweden and Prussia. The Swedes also invited the Cossacks and Transylvanians to join them. They raided deep into Poland-Lithuania. The Swedish king was able to recapture Warsaw.

The Cossacks and Transylvanians were subject to the Ottomans, and the Ottomans were angered that they had become involved in a war without their permission. They ordered the Crimean Tartars to attack them.

The Habsburg Austrians were alarmed by Sweden's success. John II Casimir led another Polish-Lithuanian counterattack. Prussia changed sides and joined the Poles under the stipulation that it was no longer a vassal of the commonwealth.

The Swedes began an ill-advised war with Denmark, and by 1660, the Polish-Lithuanian Commonwealth had retaken vast areas of Poland and the Grand Duchy of Lithuania from Sweden. However, much of the Grand Duchy of Lithuania and Vilnius remained in Russian hands. Tsar Alexei I ordered another invasion of the commonwealth. However, the large Russian army advanced based on faulty intelligence and was destroyed by the Poles and Lithuanians.

The Grand Duchy of Lithuania was devasted after the Deluge and lost up to one-third of its territories to the Russians. It was greatly reduced in size and found it increasingly difficult to field an army. The nobles grew in strength, even the treacherous Radziwiłłs, and the poor serfs became even more oppressed. Because of the Deluge, the Polish-Lithuanian Commonwealth lost its status as a great power. The power of the nobles meant that Poland and Lithuania could not initiate the reforms needed to modernize the state and army, which led it to become increasingly vulnerable.

Before the duchy could recover, another massive war took place. This was known as the Great Northern War (1701-1721). Under King Charles XII, whom historians widely considered a military genius, defeated Peter the Great at Narva in 1702. Like his predecessor Charles X, he invaded and occupied much of the grand duchy and Poland. Sweden invaded Lithuania via the Duchy of Courland, which it had occupied since the Deluge. They quickly captured Vilnius. Lithuania once more became a protectorate of the Swedes.

Locals appreciated the rule of Charles XII. However, a faction of Lithuanian nobles continued to resist Charles XII and allied with the Russians. Charles XII was defeated by Tsar Peter the Great of Russia at the Battle of Poltava after the Swedes' Cossack allies failed to support them during an invasion of Russia in 1709, marking a turning point in the Great Northern War. The defeat of the Swedes led to the reintegration of the Grand Duchy of Lithuania into the commonwealth, but again, more lands were lost.

Peter the Great and Russia became the dominant power in the Baltic region for the first time, which was symbolized by the construction of the new city of St. Petersburg. Lithuania remained a separate entity and had its own court and bureaucracy, but it was very weakened and vulnerable. Aristocratic factions fought any attempt to reform the duchy, contributing to its decline. The Lithuanians were too afraid of the Russians to seek the restoration of their independence and accepted a subordinate status in the Polish-Lithuanian Commonwealth.

Years of Stagnation

During the 18th century, Lithuania was vulnerable to internal dissent and external pressure. A contested succession led to the War of the Polish Succession (1733-1738). In general, the commonwealth stagnated and was at the mercy of its neighbors. It did not take part in the major conflicts of the time, such as the Seven Years' War (1756-1763). Poland-Lithuania was the "sick man of Europe"; its army had fallen from 160,000 to 100,000 by the late 18th century. Its economy suffered, as its raw materials were no longer in great demand in western Europe. The Polish-Lithuanian elite, who gained their wealth based on their serfs' labor, adopted the French culture.

Feudalism, which had been largely abandoned in western Europe by 1600, still flourished in eastern Europe. The feudal system that prevailed in Lithuanian lands meant that the serfs could not better themselves, and no significant middle class developed, unlike in western Europe. Trading in the towns and cities remained in the hands of Germans, Poles, and Jews. This led to ethnic tensions between the serfs and the urban population.

Remarkably, Lithuanian was not one of the official languages of the commonwealth, though it was widely spoken. Regional and ethnic divisions between the Lithuanians remained strong, but there was a strong national identity based on the glories of the past. In the towns and aristocratic circles, ideas from the West became well known, such as the abolition of serfdom, and newspapers became popular.

The Jews of Lithuania in the Commonwealth Era

The duchy had a sizeable Jewish population by the 17th century. Jews fleeing the Cossacks sought sanctuary in cities like Vilnius. Lithuanian Jews suffered greatly because of the wars that ravaged their land in the Deluge. The Lithuanian nobility allowed the Jews to set up their own legal courts, and the community was autonomous under their theocratic government. By the 1700s, they controlled a significant amount of the commerce of the duchy, which led to growing resentment. Many Jewish traders and artisans were in debt to the Lithuanian nobility. The Jews set up religious schools and were open to ideas from the West via German and Polish communities. Lithuania became a center of Jewish learning in the 17th and 18th centuries, and the judgment of rabbis influenced the development of Judaic religious law.

Vilnius, or Vilna, became one of the leading religious and cultural centers of Judaism in the early modern period. Elijah ben Solomon Zalman (1720-1779) was known as the Vilna Gaon or the genius from Vilnius. He was widely regarded as one of the most outstanding scholars of Jewish laws and an expert on the Talmud. Today, he is seen as a leader of the Misnagdim, the movement that opposed the rise of Hasidism in the late 18th and early 19th centuries. The Misnagdim, closely associated with Lithuanian Jews (Litvaks), emphasized a highly intellectual approach to the study of the Torah and the Talmud. This tradition has profoundly influenced modern Orthodox Judaism, particularly its focus on rigorous scholarship.

Despite the teachings of the Vilna Gaon, Hasidism became influential in Lithuania. Prominent Hasidic dynasties and scholars were active in Lithuania. The tolerant policies of the commonwealth and the duchy allowed for the flourishing of Jewish communities, which greatly contributed to modern Judaism. It is estimated that by the end of the 18th century, some 250,000 Jews lived in Lithuanian lands.

Tartars: Lithuanian Muslims

As the Grand Duchy of Lithuania grew into an empire, it met the Tartars, who mostly spoke a Turkic language and were Muslims. They were sometimes allies and sometimes enemies. Groups of Tartars received land in the duchy. A number of them settled in Trakai and eventually formed a quarter in Vilnius.

Remarkably, for the early modern period, the Tartars had complete religious freedom and even mosques. The Tartar elite eventually integrated into the Lithuanian nobility and governed the general Tartar population, who lived in large estates.

In general, the Tartars served in the military and became renowned as great horsemen. In return, they secured land grants. For decades, a Tartar-Lithuanian regiment was among the elite forces of the Lithuanian army. They also served as diplomats and couriers, and in the cities of the duchy, they specialized in leatherworking. In the 16th century, the last khan of the Golden Horde was held prisoner in Lithuania, and his family eventually became very prominent in Lithuanian affairs.

The Partition of Poland-Lithuania

In the aftermath of the War of the Polish Succession, the neighboring powers of Austria, Prussia, and Russia began interfering in the commonwealth. They used factions of nobles to keep it weak and divided. Russia controlled several nobles in Lithuania and Poland. Some Orthodox Christians felt they had been discriminated against by the Catholic majority. In the 1760s, the Russians began to occupy Lithuanian lands; the pretext was the need to protect Orthodox Christians, even though most were content to be part of Lithuania. This led to the formation of the Bar Confederation (1768-1772), a group of mainly Polish nobles that sought to end Russian influence in the Polish-Lithuanian Commonwealth. The regular Russian army easily beat them. As this was happening, the peasant uprising known as the Koliivshchyna occurred in what is now Ukraine and led to the massacre of non-Orthodox Christians and Jews.

The growing Russian influence in the commonwealth worried many that it would upset the balance of power in Europe. A diplomatic solution was found at the expense of the Poles and Lithuanians. The First Partition of Poland, signed in Vienna in 1772, gave lands to Prussia and Austria, and the commonwealth became a Russian puppet state. The partition was accepted by many Lithuanian nobles, as they feared the Russians and wanted to keep their estates.

Nevertheless, the first partition led to resentment among both Poles and Lithuanians. When the Russians and their allies were fighting the Swedes and the Ottoman Turks, the so-called Great Sejm was held from 1788 to 1792, and it sought to reform the commonwealth. The liberal and patriot factions were deeply influenced by the French Revolution, which started in 1789. This led to the adoption of the first constitution in Europe; among other things, it enfranchised the middle class and transformed the commonwealth into a constitutional monarchy with checks and balances. The May Constitution of 1791 would have turned the Polish-Lithuanian Commonwealth into the most democratic state of its time.

Catherine the Great of Russia was angered by this, and so were conservative pro-Russian Polish and Lithuanian magnates, who formed the Targowica Confederation. Russian forces invaded Lithuania in support of the Targowica Confederation and easily defeated the commonwealth's army. Russia and Prussia partitioned the commonwealth further in 1793, and Lithuania lost all of its old territories and was reduced to its historic area, which is similar to the modern state of Lithuania. Even the Targowica Confederation was appalled by the loss of territory.

The Poles and Lithuanians believed that the king had capitulated too quickly and wanted to fight on. They had the support of most of the population. Tadeusz Kościuszko (1746–1817) was born in the Grand Duchy of Lithuania and served with the Patriots in the American War of Independence. A brilliant military engineer, his work on fortifications, such as at West Point, helped the Continental Army. Kościuszko led the Poles and Lithuanians against the Russians and won some early victories despite being outnumbered. In the Proclamation of Połaniec (1794), Kościuszko freed the serfs and gave them political rights and equality before the law.

However, a huge Russian army invaded the commonwealth and recaptured Vilnius in August 1794. The great Russian general Alexander Suvorov defeated the rebels at the Battle of Praga and seized Warsaw, which effectively ended the revolt. In 1795, the last king of Poland and grand duke of Lithuania, Stanisław August Poniatowski, was forced to abdicate.

Russia, Prussia, and Austria divided up what was left of the commonwealth in the Third Partition of Poland in 1795. The Grand Duchy of Lithuania was no longer there and lost all independence. Now, Lithuania was merely a Russian district and had no political representation. In 150 years, beginning with the Deluge, Lithuania had gone from a grand duchy with autonomy and a partner in a mighty empire to a conquered province of imperial Russia.

Chapter Seven – From Russian Tyranny to Independence

First Years of Russian Rule

The year 1795 was a traumatic one for Lithuania. It had lost many of its historic territories and the last vestiges of its once far-flung empire. The union with Poland was broken after almost four hundred years, and many of its prized freedoms were at risk. There was never again to be a duke of Lithuania.

The decline and fall of Lithuania had been dramatic. The 19th century was to usher in a new era of struggles for Lithuanians as they fought for their national identity and political freedom.

In 1796, Tsar Paul I of Russia issued a decree that established the Lithuanian governorate and appointed a Russian governor to rule the area. Its capital was Vilnius. Russian law and administrative practices were introduced, and the power, if not the wealth, of the magnates was limited. The Lithuanian governorate was further divided into two governorates in 1801, effectively dividing historic Lithuanian populations.

At first, it might have seemed to the peasantry that they had exchanged one distant monarch for another. The Russians respected local arrangements and customs, and Lithuanian serfs had more rights than their counterparts in the rest of the Russian Empire but not much, as many suffered whippings and other forms of brutal treatment at the hands of their owners.

Things gradually began to get worse under the regime of Alexander I, as Russian law was introduced into Lithuanian lands. Russian serfdom was more severe, and a serf had even fewer rights. Many Lithuanians were conscripted into the army, and serfs could be sold, so they had to provide even more unpaid duties for their lords and the local government. Typically, the Russian authorities were corrupt and callous and only spoke Russian, causing major problems for the average Lithuanian. Most of the elite continued to enjoy many freedoms and a lavish lifestyle off the backs of the serfs. The Lithuanian economy increasingly began to stagnate as it was integrated into the Russian economy, and trade with western Europe was diminished.

Lithuania and the Napoleonic Wars

Napoleon Bonaparte's seizure of power in France in 1799 brought a new and bloody phase to the wars between the existing imperial powers and revolutionary France. The new French consul, who became emperor in 1804, was a military genius. After his stunning victory at Austerlitz in 1805, he dominated Europe. Napoleon and Tsar Alexander signed the Treaty of Tilsit in 1807 on the Neman River, which was the traditional border of Lithuanian lands. This peace treaty did not last long. Napoleon crossed the river and first entered Lithuania during his invasion of Russia in 1812. There was little fighting in Lithuania.

The French emperor established the Lithuanian Provisional Governing Commission to rule Lithuania. It was directed to create a Lithuanian army, provide provisions to the French, and administer the area. In a bid to win the support of the Lithuanians, Napoleon reestablished the grand duchy, but there was no grand duke. The French restored much of the area once ruled by the grand dukes to Lithuania. However, serfdom was not abolished, as the French wanted to secure the support of the landed aristocracy and the great families like the Radziwiłłs. Technically, Lithuania was reunited with the Duchy of Warsaw, established by Napoleon, but it was dominated by the French.

Many Lithuanians welcomed Napoleon and hoped he would help them to secure independence. Lithuanian Tartars formed a regiment, and they served with the French, who rated them highly. The governing commission raised several regiments, which were trained by Polish officers, and they all served with Napoleon. By the winter of 1812, the emperor had seized Moscow, but he found it deserted by the Russians, who continued to fight. The brutal cold and stretched supply lines forced the French to retreat, and the Russians, especially the Cossacks, harassed them mercilessly. Napoleon's army suffered horrendous casualties.

Lithuania had some sporadic anti-Russian resistance after the tsar's army recaptured the duchy, but this was suppressed with many atrocities. In the peace negotiations that ended the Napoleonic Wars, the Lithuanian city of Memel and some territories were added to Prussia. Serfdom in those lands was soon abolished. The rest of Lithuania was again attached to the Kingdom of Poland, which was nothing but a client state of Moscow.

A member of the Lithuanian Tartar Imperial Guard.[6]

Russification of Lithuania

The Russians began a campaign of Russification, which meant the erasure of all forms of Lithuanian national and cultural identity. Imperial authorities claimed that the Lithuanians were Russians who had been victims of Polonization. As part of this campaign, the Russians repressed the Lithuanian language and censored books in the language. The Catholic Church also suffered repression; many churches were destroyed or handed over to the Orthodox Church.

In 1830, the Poles rose in rebellion to win their freedom from the tsars. This, in turn, led to a revolt in the former lands of the grand duchy. The revolt in Lithuania was much smaller than the one in Poland, and the insurgents were easily defeated. In the aftermath of the revolt, many Lithuanian nobles had their estates seized and given to Russians.

The revolt in Lithuania is remarkable because of the story of Emilia Platter, born in Vilnius, who became one of the leaders of the revolt. Her strong personality allowed her to take command of a small band of insurgents. After their defeat, she refused to retreat to Prussia, where she would have been interred. She vowed to fight on, and she died of an illness in 1831. She is regarded as a national hero not only in Lithuania but also in Belarus and Poland. Emilia is often called the Lithuanian Joan of Arc.

The campaign of Russification continued with new ferocity after the revolt of 1830 under the brutal governorship of Mikhail Muravyov-Vilensky known as the "Hangman" (1796-1866). Many Lithuanian books were banned, and the University of Vilnius was closed. The imperial authorities launched a propaganda campaign to show the peasantry that they were Russians.

Catholic priests and Lithuanian intellectuals led the opposition, and they formed private schools that taught their language. They even smuggled books that had been printed abroad into the country. Gradually, at least among intellectuals, there was a recognition that all they could hope for was the reestablishment of a Lithuanian state based on an ethnic Lithuanian population and that the old lands in Belarus and Ukraine were gone forever.

Once again, a revolt in Poland sparked an anti-Russian revolt in Lithuania. On February 1st, 1863, the Lithuanians launched a bid for freedom; many of them had been in exile and returned to liberate their homeland. The Lithuanians failed to seize any towns and fought a guerrilla war. The large serf population was too oppressed to join the rebels, and their revolt finally ended in 1864.

First Stirrings of Independence

In the aftermath of the suppression of the Lithuanian and Polish revolts in 1864, a new bout of Russification began. However, in 1863, Tsar Nicholas I of Russia abolished serfdom in the Russian Empire, so the bonded class in Lithuania was technically liberated. They remained under the socioeconomic domination of their landlords and remained pitifully poor, though.

After the suppression of the 1863-1864 revolt, many Lithuanians became more interested in their history, culture, and language, like many other people in the Russian Empire, such as the Finns. A new literate class, whose members often came from a rural background, was at the forefront of this movement. The idea of the grand duchy and its former glory inspired many of these nationalists. Countless poems and novels were written celebrating the victories of Lithuania's past.

The increasingly literate people avidly read these publications. Newspapers, which were clandestinely published, were widely read in the Lithuanian language. In 1891, the Russian authorities lifted the ban on the Lithuanian language, as the ban had not been effective. Many Lithuanians spoke Polish, and the emphasis on the Lithuanian language led to divisions. Multilingualism was the norm, and many Polish-speaking Lithuanians saw themselves as both Poles and Lithuanians. In the 20th century, many would have to identify as either Poles or Lithuanians, leading to conflict.

By 1900, the tsarist government had weakened, and violent revolutionaries were trying to overthrow the system. In the rural areas of Russia, peasant revolts became an annual event. By the early 20th century, there was a host of radical and revolutionary societies operating in Lithuania, such as the Mensheviks. Still, nationalist opponents of the regime were by far the most popular.

As the Lithuanian economy began to develop, there was a measure of industrialization, and strikes and industrial unrest became common. However, most of the population lived in the countryside, worked in agriculture, and were generally better off than others in the Russian Empire.

In the 19th century, the towns of Lithuania had large numbers of Germans, Poles, and Jews who remained influential in finance and business. The Jewish population continued to grow, and while many adopted a modern lifestyle, many remained very traditional. The Hasidic movement grew in strength as a result. The old grand duchy lands were part of the Pale of Settlement, where Jews could live without having to seek official permission and on a permanent basis.

Lithuanian Exiles

In 1865, a massive wave of Lithuanians left the region, looking to escape poverty and Russian oppression. Emigration was technically illegal, and emigrants had to bribe officials or make their way to the German border secretly. Some 700,000 Lithuanians left for America and Canada. These emigrants settled in industrial areas such as Pennsylvania and worked in the factories and mines. They formed communities around Catholic and Lutheran churches and formed informal support networks. Today, millions of Americans have some heritage from the Baltic country.

There were distinct Lithuanian communities in many American cities until the 1960s. Many emigrants from the old Grand Duchy went to Australia, the United Kingdom, Brazil, and other areas of the Russian Empire; they often actively promoted the idea of Lithuanian independence.

Many Jews from Lithuania also emigrated to America. Many desired to flee the pervasive anti-Semitism in the Russian Empire and to take advantage of new economic opportunities. Many famous American Jews had some Lithuanian heritage, such as the bandleader Benny Goodman and Bob Dylan's maternal grandparents.

Even before the emergence of Zionism, many Lithuanian Jews moved to Palestine and founded religious schools. Zionist ideas found fertile ground among the Baltic region's Jews, and in the early 20th century, many moved to what would become the modern state of Israel.

Global War and Revolution

The Japanese military defeated the tsar's army in 1905, which led to a revolution. There were widespread strikes and demonstrations in Vilnius, Kaunas, and other Lithuanian cities. To end the revolt, Tsar Nicholas II agreed to reforms and allowed elections to the Duma or Parliament. The Great Seimas, a popular assembly that demanded more autonomy, was held in Vilnius. New political parties were formed, such as the Social Democrats. However, the tsar broke his promise and restored autocracy. The Great Seimas was suppressed. Nevertheless, the Great Seimas had given hope to Lithuanian nationalists.

The death of Archduke Franz Ferdinand in Sarajevo in August 1914 plunged Europe into the abyss. In the fall of 1914, the Russian army invaded Prussia from Lithuania and seized large tracts of territory. Field Marshal Paul Hindenburg launched a counterattack and defeated the Russians decisively at Tannenberg, pushing them back to Lithuania. In 1915, the Germans moved men and equipment from the Western Front to Prussia, and after a feint, they attacked Lithuanian territory as they crossed the Neman River. The Russians fell back, especially after the German capture of Warsaw in 1915. Lithuanians served in both armies, and many ethnic Lithuanians still lived in Prussia at this time.

The fighting in Lithuania was more mobile than on the Western Front, and there was little trench warfare. Local civilians suffered greatly, and whole areas of Lithuania became depopulated wastelands. The famous forests were cut down for fuel, and many were saved from starvation with aid from relatives in America and elsewhere. The parts of Lithuania occupied by the Germans were governed by the military, and despite attempts to win the locals over, they failed because they promoted local Germans. By 1916, much of Lithuania was in the hands of the Germans, including Vilnius.

The so-called February Revolution of 1917 deposed the last Russian tsar, and Alexander Kerensky succeeded him with a civilian government. The constant German assaults caused the Russian army to slowly disintegrate. In March 1917, soldiers began to mutiny and desert in substantial numbers. The leader of the revolutionary government, Kerensky, refused to end the war and ordered another offensive, which only resulted in the near collapse of the Russian army.

In October 1917, the Bolsheviks, led by Vladimir Lenin, seized power, leading to the world's first communist government. The Bolsheviks desperately needed peace and signed the Treaty of Brest-Litovsk. This meant the new Russian government recognized the independence of many of their western provinces, including Lithuania. This ended WWI on the Eastern Front, but Russia became embroiled in a civil war between the Reds (Communists) and their enemies, the Whites, who opposed the revolution.

Nationalists in Lithuania began to create their own state free from Russia. Germany supported this, as it believed the Baltic people would eventually become its protectorate. A national council, presided over by Jonas Basanavičius, called for independence and submitted a petition to the Germans declaring a new Lithuanian state. Berlin had moved many units to the Western Front, and the German soldiers trod carefully. They hoped to make the proposed new state a monarchy and the Kaiser the new head of state. To sidestep this, the national council offered the crown to a German Catholic royal, Wilhelm Karl Herzog von Urach (1864-1928). He was duly elected as king of Lithuania. This was a genius move, as the national council knew that the Germans could not oppose a German becoming monarch.

The new king, Mindaugas II, did not have a coronation. By the autumn of 1918, everyone knew the Germans were losing. On November 11th, 1918, the Germans agreed to an armistice with the Allies, and among its terms was the termination of the Treaty of Brest-Litovsk. This transformed the situation. Lithuania was on its own and had to fight for its own independence.

War of Independence

Lithuania took control of its affairs after the Germans left. The new nation had to fight for its independence in a series of wars known to the Lithuanians as the Freedom Struggles. The national government was headed by Augustinas Voldemaras (1883-1942). He declared the new country's neutrality and proclaimed that there would be no Lithuanian armed forces. He also committed his country to the pursuit of democracy, freedom, and liberty. Soon, it became clear that the new nation faced multiple threats, and it received German assistance in creating a volunteer army. Eventually, conscription was introduced.

When the Germans finally left Vilnius, a Polish, communist, and Lithuanian government all claimed to be in control of the city. Lithuanian Communists, who took orders from the Bolsheviks in Russia, set up a soviet, and the Red Army invaded from the east. The first Lithuanian government fled to Kaunas; this is considered the start of the Soviet-Lithuanian War (December 1918–August 1919). Overwhelmed, the Lithuanian army retreated, but the Poles and former German soldiers launched attacks against the advancing Soviets. Their governments did not want the Bolsheviks seizing Lithuania. The nationalists adopted partisan tactics and, with the support of the

Germans, rolled back the Bolsheviks, who had seized Vilnius and declared the Lithuanian Soviet Socialist Republic. The nationalists had the support of the population. They surrounded Vilnius and eventually retook it. They managed to push the Soviets out of Lithuania by August 1919. This was a remarkable achievement by the new state.

The danger had not passed, though. Across Russia, there were bands of armed men out of control. The Germans had created the West Russian Army out of former prisoners of war, and members of the Freikorps joined them. They were brigades of German WWI veterans, and they operated in the Baltic with the covert support of Berlin, which hoped to turn the new Baltic states—Lithuania, Latvia, and Estonia—into German dependencies. Taking advantage of the Soviet-Lithuanian fighting, the West Russian Army invaded the new state. They seized several towns and treated the civilian population brutally. The newly formed Lithuanian army was able to defeat them in a series of counterattacks and was able to drive them back to Latvia. A French force overseeing the evacuation of German troops also intervened and prevented further attacks by the West Russian Army.

The Polish-Lithuanian War

The wider region was in a state of chaos. National identities and borders were not fixed. Poland had defeated the Soviet invasion of 1920. The nationalist Polish government believed they had a right to a substantial proportion of Lithuania based on agreements going back to the Second Partition of the Polish-Lithuanian Commonwealth. In October 1920, the Poles and Lithuanians agreed to prevent a conflict. As Polish forces pushed back the Russians during their 1920 campaign, they occupied Vilnius and surrounding territories. General Lucjan Żeligowski, with covert backing from Józef Piłsudski, staged a mutiny in October 1920, leading Polish forces to seize Vilnius and declare it part of the Republic of Central Lithuania. Lithuania refused to relinquish its historic capital, sparking hostilities. Polish forces, supported by superior numbers and coordination, retained control over Vilnius, halting their advances short of Kaunas after a ceasefire was brokered in November 1920.

The League of Nations attempted to mediate the dispute but failed to reach a resolution. Lithuania lost Vilnius and its surrounding territories, which were later annexed by Poland in 1922, further straining relations between the two nations.

In 1920, the League of Nations took a strip of territory known as Memel in German and Klaipėda in Lithuanian in eastern Prussia. The League of Nations administrated it as part of an international mandate. This area was home to Prussian Lithuanians, and they wanted to unite with Lithuania. They revolted against the League of Nations and demanded unification with Lithuania. After some brief fighting in what became known as the Klaipėda Revolt in February 1923, the League of Nations granted the territory to Lithuania. Many internationally saw it as compensation for Lithuania's loss of Vilnius and the Sulwaki region.

Lithuanian, a Nation Once Again

After over a century of tyranny, the Lithuanians had emerged triumphant. They had retained their national identity and had regained their freedom. Yet, the new state was only a shadow of the Lithuania of the past, and it was very weak. An independent Lithuania was about to enter a period filled with challenges. It was devastated by war and surrounded by often hostile enemies, and the various minorities in the new republic were all restive.

Chapter Eight – Hitler, Stalin, and the Holocaust

From Republic to Dictatorship

The new Lithuanian Republic was a liberal democracy and drew up its constitution based on the principles of freedom and equality. The international community recognized Poland's claim of Vilnius, but the new Lithuanian government refused to accept this. This led to a breakdown in relations with Warsaw, which affected the economy. It could not hold an election until 1923 because of threats from Poland.

The Constituent Assembly ruled the country and introduced much-needed land reforms, a new currency, and other innovations. A final constitution was agreed to by the Constituent Assembly in 1922. The first general elections produced the first parliament based on the constitution, the Seimas, in 1923, but it was deeply divided between left-wing and right-wing parties. The political parties were all deeply divided despite being Lithuanian nationalists.

The success of the Klaipėda Revolt was critical for the country in 1920. This was the successful bid by Lithuanians in Klaipėda (Memel) to unify with Lithuania. The incorporation of this territory allowed the new state more access to the Baltic Sea after the loss of Vilnius to the Poles.

The country was divided not only by politics but also on the grounds of ethnicity. After independence, Lithuania had significant minorities of Poles and Jews, and in the Klaipėda area, the Germans were in the majority (they called it Memel).

The Second Seimas was dominated by the Christian Democrats, a center-right party that introduced a series of moderate reforms, such as social insurance based on the Swedish model. They also secured a majority in the Third Seimas in 1926. A minority Christian Democratic government signed a treaty with the Soviet Union, but this was very unpopular. Many on the right accused them of caving into the communists. The chief critic of the government was the Lithuanian Nationalist Union, a right-wing popular movement. The army deposed the government in 1926 in a coup and ended democracy, which was common in Eastern Europe during the interwar period.

Antanas Smetona (1874-1944), the first president of Lithuania, became president again. He ruled in an authoritarian manner. He even developed a cult of personality, and his party, the Lithuanian Nationalist Union, was able to dominate the assembly. In theory, Lithuania was a democracy, but it was an authoritarian state. Smetona repressed his opposition, harassed the press, and curtailed the rights of ethnic minorities. The authoritarian government was faction-riven and could not introduce any new reforms.

The Wall Street Crash of 1929 led to the Great Depression, leading to a severe economic downturn in Lithuania. The rise of Hitler in Germany led to tensions with Berlin over Memel. The Nazis stoked German agitation in the region and even imposed a trade embargo on Lithuanian goods. In 1938, the Polish government issued an ultimatum to Lithuania concerning diplomatic relations, which Smetona was forced to accept. Lithuania was trapped between an aggressive Poland, Germany, and the Soviet Union. During the 1920s and 1930s, the urban centers became dominated by ethnic Lithuanians for the first time, and the country was stable.

In 1939, Nazi Germany and the Soviet Union signed the Ribbentrop-Molotov Pact, which effectively partitioned Central and Eastern Europe between them. Lithuania was granted to the Soviet Union through the pact. In November 1938, the Soviets forced the Poles to return Vilnius to Lithuania. However, the Soviets began to flagrantly interfere in the republic. After an ultimatum in 1940, President Smetona fled, and his country was occupied by a force of 150,000 Soviet soldiers.

Soviet Occupation (1940-1941)

After only twenty years of independence, Lithuania was once again under the control of Russia, albeit under a new political system, communism. Moscow set up a new puppet soviet state in Lithuania under the collaborator Justas Paleckis (1899–1980). The Lithuanian population, with exceptions, hated the communists. Only a tiny minority welcomed them.

Stalin rigged the elections of 1940, and a left-wing coalition was placed in power that was answerable to him. Soon, political parties were banned, and the press was tightly controlled. Stalin initially moved slowly. He broke up large estates and gave land to the peasants, a move that was popular. In other areas, the Soviets moved fast and began the Sovietization of the Lithuanian state. Stalin withdrew the Lithuanian currency from circulation, resulting in an economic depression exacerbated by the nationalization of industry and the banks. By late 1940, all political, cultural, and social organizations had been banned. Membership of the Communist Party was now mandatory for any public servant. Lithuanian soldiers had to serve in the Soviet Army. Stalin began to persecute religious groups, places of worship were shut down, and a campaign of propaganda was launched to discredit religion. Stalin wanted to eradicate all forms of Lithuanian national identity.

The Soviet secret police began to terrorize the population. Opponents or imagined opponents of the regime faced arrest during the night. They were tortured and sometimes secretly executed. Twelve thousand people were arrested, and many were deported to Siberia for crimes such as being a Boy Scout or having a national emblem. In June 1941, Stalin ordered the mass deportation of alleged "enemies of the people" from the Baltic states to the Gulag in Siberia. This was an attempt to ensure that the Baltic people could not resist Sovietization.

Invasion and War

In June 1941, Hitler launched the invasion of the Soviet Union despite the Ribbentrop-Molotov Pact. German armed units crossed the Neman River and advanced deep into Lithuania. The Soviets retreated, but as they did, they committed crimes, such as the Rainiai massacre. Army Group North of the German army soon defeated the surprised Soviet units, which sparked a revolt among Lithuanians, who attacked the retreating enemy. The rebels, often deserters from the Soviet Army, seized Vilnius and declared the independence of their homeland.

After the initial shock, the Soviets launched a counterattack. On June 23rd, two Soviet Tank Corps attacked German Panzer units crossing the Neman. This resulted in a four-day tank battle. Soviet KV-1 and KV-2 tanks inflicted heavy losses on the invaders, but the Red Army had to retreat, suffering the loss of 750 tanks. After this battle, the Germans controlled all of the Lithuanian territories. Many Lithuanians welcomed the Germans as liberators after the horrors inflicted on them by the Soviets, and many dreamed of independence. However, they were replacing one dictatorship with another.

Initially, the Germans tolerated the Lithuanian government, but they later replaced it with a military regime. Lithuanians largely worked with the regime, but at times, they opposed Nazi policies, which led them to be sent to concentration camps. Lithuania had to provide supplies and men to the Nazi war machine, which caused great misery.

The Holocaust in Lithuania

The Baltic nation had a Jewish population of 200,000 to 220,000 in 1939, which was concentrated in the urban centers. There had long been a history of anti-Semitism in Lithuania, but in general, the Jewish community had thrived, even under the authoritarian regime of Smetona. However, as the Lithuanian rebels began to attack the Soviets in June 1941, groups of them began to viciously attack the Jewish communities, which were often mistakenly believed by right-wingers to be communists. It appears that many nationalist groups spread propaganda about the Jews and that the Nazis sponsored their attacks. Subsequent historians have found that many Lithuanians collaborated with the Germans in their campaign to exterminate the Jews, much more so than in other countries, but this is controversial.

The Holocaust in Lithuania is remarkable for the speed of the destruction of its Jews. Most of them were killed by the end of 1941; in other words, a large number were killed in about six months. Local paramilitary units started pogroms targeting their Jewish neighbors. The militia commander Algirdas Klimaitis organized his men, and they attacked the Jewish population in Kaunas on June 25th. Their victims were often attacked in the middle of the night, and many were brutally murdered and raped. Synagogues were burned to the ground. The anti-Semitic violence spread to other towns, and thousands of Jews died in the pogroms. Most of these killings were directly attributed to Lithuanian collaborators such as Iron Wolf, a Lithuanian paramilitary organization.

Survivors of the Skaudvilė pogrom told a court in 1961 that they witnessed pregnant women being stabbed in their bellies and children having their brains bashed out with the support of the Germans. Some of the collaborators were criminals who simply attacked the Jews so that they could steal their property. There is some evidence that many collaborators helped the Nazis in the belief that they would look favorably on a proposal for a new Lithuanian state.

Most of the killings of the Holocaust in Lithuania were carried out by the Germans through the Einsatzgruppen; these were paramilitary units under the command of the SS. They were often volunteers, and they were, in effect, death squads. They were entrusted with killing all of the enemies of the Nazis in the newly occupied lands. The Einsatzgruppen committed many massacres in Poland. They were assisted in their killings by the regular German police. In Lithuania, local collaborators helped them target Jews, and this is believed to have allowed the Einsatzgruppen to kill more of their victims more efficiently.

While the Einsatzgruppen killed individuals on an ad-hoc basis, they usually went about their task with brutal efficiency. They would cordon off a Jewish neighborhood or town and order all the Jews to leave their possessions behind and follow them. They were told that they were being relocated. Typically, the Germans forced them to travel to a remote area and made them strip naked before they were shot and thrown into a pit. In one massacre, some nine thousand Jews from Kovno were murdered, and their bodies were thrown in trenches. Whole communities were destroyed in this way.

The activities involving the death squads and the pogroms continued until Christmas of 1941. Academics believe that up to half of the Jewish community perished at this time. However, not all Lithuanians helped the Nazis, and some helped Jews to escape or hide.

Germans and Lithuanian collaborators burning down a synagogue.[7]

After 1941, the rate of killings slowed, as the Nazis needed the labor of the Jews. The German authorities established ghettoes or open-air prisons in the cities of Vilna, Kovno, and Siauliai, among others, which were run by Jewish councils set up by the Germans. Many Jews were then transported to labor camps to work as slaves. The conditions in the ghettoes and camps were appalling, and a considerable number of Jews died of hunger and disease or from the guards' brutal treatment. In Kovno, the large Jewish population was forced to live in a few streets and made to work, even the children and elderly. In 1943, the Germans closed the Vilnius and Kovno ghettoes, and the able-bodied inhabitants were sent to other labor camps. The weak and old were transported to be gassed at Auschwitz. The Kovno and Siauliai ghettos were converted into concentration camps where Jews and others were worked to death.

This situation continued until the spring of 1944 when the Germans retreated from the Soviets. To hide their crimes and to address their labor needs, the Germans transported surviving Jews to concentration camps in Germany and Poland. Here, countless more died. In 1945, as the Soviets advanced, the Germans ordered the evacuation of these camps, and the Jews were forced on death marches.

There are no accurate statistics on the number of Jews killed by the Germans and their local collaborators, but the Jewish population fell by about 90 percent, although some Jews might have emigrated and escaped death. The death rate among the Jewish community was the highest of any country that suffered Nazi tyranny. Today, there is only a tiny Jewish population, and it is aging fast. They are the last remnants of what was once one of the centers of the Jewish diaspora.

It should be noted that Jews were not the only victims of the Holocaust in the Baltic nation. For example, thousands of Poles and Soviet prisoners of war died at the hands of the Nazis during the Ponary massacre outside Vilnius in 1941.

Resistance and Collaboration

Germany had plans for Lithuania. In the racial hierarchy, Lithuanians were inferior to Aryan Germans, and their lands had to be confiscated, and the population enslaved or deported. Lithuanians became suspicious of the Germans and refused to help them, which led to some form of resistance, usually non-cooperation or sabotage. Soviet partisans became active in the Baltic country by late 1942 under the leadership of Antanas Sniečkus. They launched hit-and-run attacks on the Nazis and the Lithuanian police that collaborated with the Germans. In the Vilnius region, Polish partisans began to fight the Germans and the local police, which led to something like a civil war in that region, with both sides committing atrocities. By 1944, whole villages were being annihilated in a series of tit-for-tat reprisals. In June 1944, the Polish Home Army, as part of its rebellion against the Nazis, attempted to seize the city of Vilnius, but they were beaten back by the garrison.

Many Jews, after the initial massacres, began to fight back against the Nazis and their local collaborators. Abba Kovner, a future acclaimed Hebrew poet, formed the United Partisan Organization. Its members attempted to raise a revolt in the Vilna Ghetto. This failed, but many Jews escaped to the forests. From there, they attacked the Nazis and their sympathizers and were amazingly effective at sabotage.

Increasingly after 1943, ethnic Lithuanians formed partisan bands, such as the Lithuanian Freedom Army. They were slow to start attacks against the Germans, but as the Soviets pressed on the borders of the country, they were emboldened and began to attack the occupation forces and their collaborators. By 1944, Lithuania was the scene of bitter fighting between collaborators and partisans.

In the early years of the occupation, many Lithuanians volunteered to join the regular German army; they were motivated to do so out of their hatred of the Soviets. Significant numbers were later conscripted into labor battalions that worked behind the front lines. The occupiers also raised self-defense units to provide security in the rear areas, but these proved to be highly unreliable.

The Lithuanians grew angry at the efforts to recruit their young men. A German campaign to recruit local young men into the Waffen-SS was boycotted, and only a few hundred served with the notorious unit. This led to reprisals against those who organized the boycott. Nevertheless, those Lithuanians who served in the German army became a source of controversy for many years after the war.

The Soviet Advance

After the great victory at the Battle of Kursk in 1943, the Soviets went on the offensive. By the fall of 1944, they were approaching the Baltic states. In August 1944, they launched an offensive against Nazi-occupied Estonia. Success here led to the Baltic offensive. A Soviet force of over one million soldiers attacked the German occupiers. Stalin ordered an offensive against Memel (Klaipėda). The seizure of this would have cut the German army in the Baltic in two. The Soviets achieved a tactical surprise, and they managed to drive the Wehrmacht (the Nazi armed forces) back to almost the Gulf of Riga and surrounded them by October 1944. As a result of this and other actions, the Germans became trapped in the Courland Peninsula, which became the so-called Courland Pocket.

Soon, much of Lithuania was in the hands of the Soviets. The Reds presented it as liberation, but to the ordinary person, it was a reoccupation. The Western Allies showed little interest in the plight of the Baltic republics and left them to the mercy of Stalin. Soviet soldiers committed countless acts of robbery and murder. Like other Eastern European countries, Lithuania did not regain its freedom at the end of WWII. It just changed one occupier for another.

Chapter Nine – Soviet Terror and Repression Post-WWII (1944–1985)

Once the Red Army had driven the Germans out of the Baltic, they began to reassert their control. In Lithuania, they set up a socialist republic. The Lithuanian Soviet Socialist Republic became one of the republics of the Soviet Union and was technically autonomous. Initially, Western governments did not recognize this and treated the existing anti-communist delegations in their countries as representatives of the legitimate government.

Stalin began the immediate Sovietization of the Baltic country. Moscow had little sympathy for the Lithuanians, as it believed they had not done enough to resist the German invaders. Sovietization was the imposition of a political and socioeconomic system based on workers' councils, and the communists enthusiastically enforced it. It involved adopting the culture, social relationships, and worldview of the Soviet Union. Russian culture was prioritized, including its language.

The Lithuanian Communists were given control of all state institutions. Loyal Lithuanian Communists, those who Stalin had not liquidated in one of his purges, were appointed to various roles. The local communists had little freedom and had to answer to many Russian advisers. Those who had worked for the previous regime suffered harassment and were often arrested.

By decree, all private property was nationalized, and the Soviets took over all industry and every economic institution. Businesspeople lost everything at the stroke of a pen. In 1947, Moscow ordered the collectivization of farms, and people in rural areas were ordered to join kolkhozes, or collective farms. Here, they worked for their rations and some money, and their lives were tightly regulated. They had to hand over a large part of their produce to the state, and they were generally poorer than before. Until 1953, they needed permission to travel outside their local area. They were not alone.

Russian became the state's official language, and it was mandatory in the schools under the Soviets. Furthermore, Lithuanian had to be written in the Cyrillic alphabet. Lithuanian culture was repressed, and Soviet culture was promoted in the media. Young people had to join the Komsomol or Young Communists, where they were indoctrinated to adopt Russian ways and the Soviet mentality. Religious groups became strictly regulated and regularly harassed. Lithuania Minor, a historical region of Lithuania, was transferred to the newly created Kaliningrad, a Soviet territory formed out of former Prussian lands. Thousands of ethnic Lithuanians who had lived in the area for centuries had to leave.

Lithuanian deportees in Siberia (possibly from the 1950s).[8]

Police State and Repression

Moscow established a police state in the Baltic countries, and the secret police, the NKVD and later the KGB, monitored people's communications and beliefs. The Soviet state intruded into every aspect of life.

From May 1945, there was a wave of deportations. Lists of "enemies of the state" were compiled, and they, along with their families, were exiled from their homeland. Lithuanian Communists collaborated in the deportation of their fellow countrymen and women. In some regions and counties, every man from eighteen to forty was arrested and sent to Siberia.

Every deportation followed a pattern. The local communists would issue an order against enemies of the states and bandits. Extra police and soldiers would be drafted into an area, and it would be cordoned off. They would conduct the operations at night and in secrecy. Those who resisted were beaten and shot. All they could take of their former life was some personal items, and the soldiers could steal these. Families were separated, and those who did manage to escape were later reported for deportation because of fears of reprisals against their families. Antanas Sniečkus (1902-1974), a Lithuanian and committed Stalinist was the most powerful politician in the Baltic state. He was instrumental in these affairs and even had family members deported.

Substantial numbers of those who were deported were sent to central Asia on journeys that often lasted weeks or even months. Deportees from Kaunas were sent to Tashkent and made to work on cotton plantations in conditions reminiscent of slavery. The Soviets arrested wealthy farmers and former landlords and sent them on trains to the Far East. The deportees endured brutal conditions, and many died on the journey to their new "home."

Stalin used the deportations to ensure Soviet rule was never challenged. In 1949, Operation Priboi transported ninety thousand people from the Baltic states to Siberia. The Reds herded whole families onto cattle trucks, and those that escaped were hunted down and summarily shot. These deportations continued until 1952. It is estimated that some 130,000 Lithuanians were deported and sent into exile; most of them were women and children. Over twenty thousand died because of the deportations.

After Stalin's death, the deportations ended. By the 1960s, many of those who had been deported received permission to return home, but thousands could not. Every year, the suffering of the deportees is remembered on Mourning and Hope Day (June 14th).

The Resistance: Brothers of the Forest (1944-1953)

Toward the end of the German occupation, the Lithuanian partisans knew that the Soviets would reoccupy their homeland and that brutal repression would follow. Anit-Soviet partisan groups were set up, and they armed themselves with old German and Soviet weapons. They developed units with a command structure and hideouts. The outnumbered partisans adopted guerrilla tactics and took to the vast forests of Lithuania. Because of this, they became known as the Forest Brothers or Brothers of the Forest. All were proud Lithuanians who were committed to fighting to the death. They usually carried a grenade that they would detonate rather than endure Soviet torture and prison.

Thousands of men took to the forest during the early weeks of the Soviet occupation, and they had the support of the population and the churches. Many of the partisans were deserters from the Red Army or had refused to be conscripted into the Red Army.

In the summer of 1944, the partisans began to attack the Soviets, who were still fighting the Germans on the Eastern Front. The Soviet high command sent inexperienced troops to destroy the Lithuanians, but they suffered heavy casualties. By the spring of 1945, the Forest Brothers had control of the forests and even remote villages, and they had created a liberated zone in Lithuania. The success of the partisans can be seen in the fact that the Soviets, who feared that they could not defeat them militarily, announced an amnesty for those who handed up their weapons and returned to civilian life.

The Soviets began to increasingly use units of the feared secret police, the NKVD. They were highly trained, experienced, and ruthless. Soviet propaganda portrayed the freedom fighters as bandits. Because of censorship, the West knew little about the Forest Brothers. Similar anti-Soviet groups became active in the other Baltic republics. Those who resisted the communists did not suffer deportation but were imprisoned or sent to a mental health facility.

After 1946, as the NKVD's presence increased in the forests after the final defeat of the Germans, the partisans changed tactics. They hid in bunkers, engaged in sabotage operations, and successfully disrupted the rigged elections to the Supreme Soviet (the highest governing body of the Lithuanian Soviet Socialist Republic). To most Lithuanians, the partisans became a symbol of hope in a dark time.

In response to the activities of the Forest Brothers, Stalin ordered more deportations. The families of suspected Forest Brothers could be arrested. Those even suspected of involvement with the partisans were routinely tortured and killed at the infamous NKVD headquarters in Vilnius. The deportations and the repression began to sap the strength of the resistance movement.

To revive the resistance movement, the patriots formed the Union of Lithuanian Freedom Fighters. This was a more centralized organization that aimed to coordinate the activities of the various groups. The new, more centralized structure was more vulnerable to infiltration and double agents.

NKVD units engaged in sweeps of the forests and villages, and the Forest Brothers became increasingly isolated. By 1953, the freedom fighters had suffered thousands of casualties and found it increasingly harder to survive in the forests. The Union of Lithuanian Freedom Fighters dissolved. Additionally, they no longer posed a significant threat to the Soviets. Even after 1953, small units of partisans continued to resist. Individual members of the Forest Brothers were still hiding in the forest as late as the 1960s. The last partisan only died in 1969; he was killed by the KGB. Lithuanians revere the memory of the Forest Brothers, and there are significant monuments to their bravery and patriotism throughout the Baltic republic.

The Lithuanian Economy and Society under the Soviets

The death of Stalin and the virtual end of the Forest Brothers' campaign led to a "thaw" in Lithuania. Repression became less severe, and more freedom was granted to those who worked on the collective farms. Under Nikita Khrushchev and Leonid Brezhnev, the Soviets continued the process of Sovietization but at a less drastic pace. They encouraged the industrialization of the economy and invested heavily in factories and mines. This, in turn, led to increasing urbanization, and the Baltic nation transformed. The infrastructure of the nation also developed, and literacy levels increased. Lithuania became one of the wealthiest states in the USSR.

Many of the developments in the Soviet period continue to benefit the Baltic country to this day. Soviet apologists like to promote the myth of a benevolent Soviet Union. Yet, others point to the fact that the Lithuanians drove the new socioeconomic developments, and what is more, the Baltic nation was a net contributor to the Soviet Union but was treated like a colony by Moscow. While the Soviets improved the rights of minorities and women, it must be noted that the Baltic country was very progressive before 1940. It is undeniable that the Soviets introduced reforms, but the political system was undemocratic and gave Russians too much influence. Corruption and cronyism became the norm. Moreover, the country became isolated from the rest of the world, and it began to stagnate economically, socially, and culturally from the 1960s onward.

The most dramatic change in the Soviet period was the change in demographics. The once-vibrant Jewish population was only a fraction of what it had been, and the few survivors of the Holocaust emigrated to Israel and America. Between 1944 and 1945, Stalin ordered the expulsion of ethnic Poles to Poland; 200,000 Poles were forced to leave. The Baltic Germans, who had lived in the urban areas since the Middle Ages, were also expelled. Soviet policy was to increase control by encouraging Russian emigration to the Baltic states. Communist officials and ordinary citizens were encouraged to settle in Lithuania, and they replaced the Jews, Germans, and Poles in the cities and towns.

There was already a Russian minority in the country, many of them White Russians who fled from the Soviets. They often lived in separate neighborhoods and had, in general, better housing and more privileges, which angered their Lithuanian neighbors. This led to tensions in parts of the country.

Antanas Sniečkus, who became the head of the Communist Party in 1940, became more nationalistic and tried to protect his fellow countrymen. He voiced concerns about the high levels of Russian emigration, and Moscow was concerned about reducing the flow of migrants. Nevertheless, the number of Russians grew, and by the 1990s, they numbered around 9 percent of the population of Lithuania. This was lower than that of neighboring Latvia, whose population of Russians and other Soviet ethnicities comprised 40 percent of the population.

Lithuania from 1953-1985: Stagnation and Sovietization

The veteran communist leader Sniečkus dominated Lithuania until he died in 1974. After his death, the Communist Party was increasingly in the hands of bureaucrats instead of revolutionaries. These bureaucrats were known as apparatchiks. These apparatchiks worked full-time for the Communist Party, had privileges, and were notoriously conservative and corrupt.

Petras Griškevičius became the head of the communist government of Lithuania in 1974, and under him, the economy gradually stagnated, and corruption worsened. He continued with the policy of Sovietization, and the Lithuanian culture and history continued to be suppressed. Those who opposed the regime faced arrest, and the communist government had countless agents and informers looking out for any anti-Soviet activities. Academics often consider the 1970s to be an era of economic stagnation, as the economy did not grow, and living standards fell. People, including communists, became disillusioned with the situation.

In 1975, the Soviets signed the Helsinki Accords on human rights, which allowed for the monitoring of human rights in Lithuania. This helped to liberalize education and the press. Intellectuals could again discuss reforms and begin to engage in nationalistic activities, such as writing about the Baltic state's history and culture. This did much to counter the Sovietization policies. They were so successful that Petras Griškevičius ordered a new program of Sovietization in Lithuanian schools. However, the Soviet elite could no longer reform the system.

The country was unable to compete with the military and technological advances of the West during the Cold War, and the Lithuanian population remained poor. After a series of elderly communists, a reformer named Mikhail Gorbachev (1931-2022) became the chairman of the Communist Party of the Soviet Union and the leader of the USSR.

Lithuanian protestor confronts Soviet tanks.⁹

Decline and Fall of Communism

Mikhail Gorbachev introduced the policies of perestroika (renewal) and glasnost (openness) between 1984 and 1986. A committed communist, he wanted to reform the system and make it work for the ordinary people. Initially, Gorbachev was exceedingly popular in the Soviet Union and especially in Lithuania. Young people began to form cultural and social organizations, often of a nationalist nature. While Lithuanians welcomed Gorbachev's reforms, they wanted more, and soon, there were talks of full independence from the Soviet Union.

By the late 1980s, the economy was collapsing because of inflation, and public discontent was growing, especially in the Baltic states. Gorbachev was reluctant to crack down on the dissent. Lithuanian intellectuals and artists formed Sąjūdis ("Movement") to seek greater freedom for the country. They began to organize rallies, petitions, and concerts to promote their cause. They collaborated with nationalists in other Baltic states, and it became known as the "Singing Revolution." In 1988, nationalists formed a human chain across the Baltic region to call for more autonomy and democracy.

In November 1989, the Berlin Wall collapsed after Gorbachev refused to intervene and prop up the puppet communist states in Eastern Europe. Free elections were held in Lithuania in 1990, and they returned a reconstituted Seimas, which was dominated by nationalists calling for independence. Lithuania declared itself to be independent from the Soviet Union in March 1990 to the astonishment of the world. This was a major event in the dissolution of Soviet control in the country and inspired other nationalist movements across the USSR. The unprecedented declaration of independence showed that Soviet rule could be challenged.

Gorbachev refused to send in the military and adopted a more subtle approach. Moscow introduced an economic embargo to punish the Baltic nation. While it caused a measure of hardship, it was ineffectual, and the Lithuanians remained committed to their freedom. The standoff continued until 1991, when Soviet soldiers were ordered to take over a local TV station that was broadcasting news that was uncensored. This led to a bloody standoff known as the January Events. Lithuanians and Soviet soldiers clashed for two days between January 11th and 13th, during which fourteen people died and hundreds were injured. The world media broadcasted these events, and the images damaged Gorbachev's reputation. The military raids and shows of force continued for some months.

In February 1991, a referendum was held, and voters supported the bid for independence by a wide margin. By this time, nationalists throughout the USSR, inspired by the Lithuanians, were demanding their autonomy or outright independence. Other Soviet republics recognized the independence of Lithuania to defy Moscow and demonstrate their right to declare independence.

Lithuania continued to assert its independence even as Soviet border guards tried to cut off the nation from the outside world. During an attempted coup by communist hardliners in August 1991, the Soviet Army occupied serval key sites in Vilnius. After mass protests in Moscow, the coup that attempted to restore the old Soviet system collapsed. Soon after, the Soviet Union began to break up, and more republics began announcing their independence. The State Council of the Soviet Union recognized Lithuania as an independent state on September 6th, 1991. After half a century of tyranny and oppression, the Baltic nation was once again free. Its role in the decline and fall of the Soviet Union was significant, and remarkably, it was because of peaceful and nonviolent protests.

Chapter Ten – Opportunities and Old Threats

The Challenges of Freedom

Lithuania was independent, but it faced considerable and deep-seated problems. Its people had been repressed economically, socially, and politically, and the scars of the Soviet era took a long time to heal.

The first government of Lithuania, led by the Movement Party (Sąjūdis), played the lead role in the quest for independence. A major issue was the economy. Lithuania, which had been integrated into the Soviet economy, was on its own. It could no longer export to the Soviet Union. This resulted in rising unemployment and inflation, causing the standard of living to fall and poverty levels to soar.

Influenced by the West, the new government adopted the tenets of neoliberalism, which led to the introduction of free market reforms. Soon after independence, the first government of an independent Lithuania introduced an ambitious program to privatize the economy. According to the data, state activity accounted for almost three-quarters of the gross domestic product (GDP) in 1990. Privatization involved the selling of all state-owned assets, such as collective farms, banks, factories, and other businesses nationalized by the Soviets after 1944. Economic advisers from America and Europe counseled the government to give citizens investment vouchers. These vouchers allowed ordinary citizens to benefit from the funds raised during privatization.

Privatization was well regulated in the country, unlike in other Soviet republics, where it was hijacked by gangsters and corrupt politicians. By 1995, much of the economy was in private hands, but this meant that the old safeguards were discarded. Unlike during the Soviet era, no one was guaranteed a job, and many people suffered. Aid and subsidies from the West did little to help. In 1993, a new Lithuanian currency, the litas, was introduced. It could be traded freely on the international market and was an important symbol of economic independence.

The shock of the free market reforms caused a socioeconomic crisis, and the governing party, Sąjūdis, became very unpopular. Former communists created the Democratic Labour Party of Lithuania, and they won the second free election held in 1993. This was a remarkable turnaround, and it shows how severe the economic crisis that gripped the country was. This was not unusual, as many former communist countries elected reformed communists to power in protest of the free market reforms introduced after the fall of communism. However, the former Lithuanian Communists were pragmatists, and the privatization program continued.

In 1996, the Democratic Labour Party's share of the vote collapsed; it only received less than 10 percent of the vote. The Democratic Labour Party of Lithuania dissolved in 2001.

Despite breaking away from the Soviet Union, the country still depended on the Russian economy. The Russian financial crisis of 1998 negatively affected the economy, and the country was forced to reorientate its economy to export to the West. By pegging the currency to the new euro, the rate of inflation fell, which helped to stabilize the economy. However, it came at a social cost.

Similar to other countries after the fall of communism, there was a great deal of social dislocation in Lithuania. Organized gangs flourished, and shootings and explosions became common in the cities and towns. There was a general sense of insecurity. Lithuanian gangs became involved in a range of criminal activities, including human trafficking, drug smuggling, prostitution, and extortion. They trafficked countless vulnerable people to Western Europe, where they were coerced into sex work or were economically exploited in a variety of ways.

Lithuanian troops in a NATO exercise.[10]

The European Union and NATO

In 2000, Lithuania received an invitation to join the European Union. There was great enthusiasm in the country for this, as the population saw it as a way to bring the country closer to Europe and the West. On May 1st, 2004, the country was formally accepted into the European Union. Lithuania gained immense economic benefits by joining, as the EU provided structural funds and aid to help the country develop. Its acceptance to the EU has resulted in the transformation of the Lithuanian economy. Its GDP is now 85 percent of the EU average in 2020, and in 2001, it was only 43 percent of the European Union average. The level of unemployment has fallen, there has been an increase in social spending by the government, and living standards have increased. Today, Lithuania is a service economy with a small but vibrant industrial sector. However, unemployment remains higher than the European average, and poverty rates are also higher.

In 2004, when Lithuania joined the EU, it became a member of the North Atlantic Treaty Organization (NATO), a mutual defense pact. It joined the world's most powerful military alliance, which was seen as essential for its future security. Lithuanian forces have served in Afghanistan along with other NATO forces. As a member of NATO, if Lithuania experiences any form of military attack, then the country will receive unqualified support from NATO's other members, including the US and the UK. For ordinary Lithuanians, this has provided a source of security, and they believe that the threat from Russia has been reduced. Still, they believe that their Eastern neighbor remains a real threat.

The expansion of NATO membership to Eastern European countries has been controversial, as it has angered the Russians and made rapprochement with the West almost impossible after the end of the Cold War.

Lithuanian Relations with the Russian Federation and Russian Minority

While the Soviet Union collapsed and tsarist Russia was history, Lithuania was still threatened by Russia. Both countries shared a common border at the Kaliningrad Oblast, which is a Russian outpost on the Baltic Sea. In the 1990s, Vilnius feared that the instability in the former Soviet Union would spill over into its territory, and Russian mafia gangs came to be seen as a threat. The presidency of Vladimir Putin, who first took office in 2000, stabilized the situation in Russia, but many in Lithuania became alarmed at his nationalist postures at an early date. Lithuania initially was able to have good relations with Russia, and in 2008, it felt confident enough to end conscription.

By the 2000s, it became apparent that Moscow would use energy to put pressure on its former satellites, which it regularly did in Ukraine. By the mid-2000s, Vilnius was still dependent on the energy provided by the Russian energy firm Gazprom, a legacy of the Soviet past when Lithuania had been integrated into the USSR's energy system. Lithuanians still retained bitter memories of the Soviet years, and in 2006, Vilnius demanded reparations for past abuses in the Baltic nation. Moscow briefly placed an embargo on diesel exports to Lithuania in retaliation.

One priority was to achieve energy independence from Moscow, and Vilnius began to diversify its energy sources and developed a strategy to achieve energy independence from Russia. In Klaipėda, a new LNG (liquefied natural gas) terminal was constructed as part of this strategy.

The Baltic nation had many monuments to the Soviet past. These had been erected to mark the glories of the communists and their "liberation" of Lithuania. Naturally, these were highly offensive to many, and starting in 1991, they were taken down. This continued for many years, and it angered Moscow.

There have been frequent cyberattacks organized by state-backed Russian hackers since the 2000s in Lithuania during periods of tension between Vilnius and Moscow, such as after the 2008 ban on Soviet symbols. This ban was seen in Russia as being disrespectful to those who died in the Great Patriotic War (WWII).

The greatest source of tension has been the large Russian minority in the Baltic state. Like its neighbors, Lithuania had a large Russian community because of Soviet-sponsored migration policies. Since 1991, many Russians have emigrated, and they now consist of around 5 percent of the population concentrated in urban areas. They have Russian-language schools and are members of the Orthodox Church, which was, until recently, under the authority of the Moscow Patriarchate, which is widely seen as an agent of the Putin regime.

At times, there have been tensions between the Lithuanians and Russians, and many ethnic Russians in the Baltic republic have even claimed that they faced some form of discrimination. There is data to suggest that they are more likely to be unemployed and experience some form of social exclusion. It has long been feared that the Putin regime may use the Russians as an excuse to launch military action against the Baltic nation.

The European Union and Emigration

A growing world economy and membership in the EU brought significant benefits to Lithuania. Its economy grew rapidly, and in the 2000s, because of its rapid rise in the GDP, Lithuanians, along with Latvians and Estonians, became known as the Baltic Tigers in the international media. The country implemented more reforms and is now ranked highly on indexes for ease of doing business. Lithuania's economy diversified and was no longer dependent on the former Soviet Union.

Despite the successes, poverty and unemployment remained an issue. Youth unemployment, in particular, was and remains high. After the Baltic nation joined the European Union, its people could live and work in any member state. For many years, young Lithuanians wanted to move west for opportunities. After 2004, there was a massive increase in emigration out of the country. This is known as the Third Wave of Emigration, and most emigrants moved to Western Europe. By 2008, there were large communities of migrants in the United Kingdom, France, Germany, Ireland, Sweden, Denmark, and the Netherlands.

At first, this had a positive impact on the economy, as remittances helped to boost local consumption, and the wave of emigration helped to reduce unemployment. However, elevated levels of emigration and a low birth rate have led to real concerns over a demographic crisis in the country. Under the Soviet Union, the birth rate declined rapidly because of improvements in women's education, and in the post-Soviet period, the economic circumstances dissuaded ordinary people from having children. As a result, the birth rate in Lithuania has been below the replacement level of 2.1 for two generations. This is regarded as one of the greatest challenges to the Baltic state. An aging society will provide significant social and economic challenges, just as it will in other societies around the globe.

Since 2020, more Lithuanians have returned to the country than have left. Nevertheless, it still remains low. The population of the Baltic nation was 3.7 million in 1990; today, it is only 2.706 million.

Lithuania and the Continuing Struggle for Freedom

Lithuania became increasingly wary of the intentions of the Putin regime, especially after its war with Georgia in 2008. Its leaders, along with those from other Eastern European countries, urged NATO and the EU to adopt a tough approach to Russia, but in general, they were ignored by Western governments like Germany, which wanted to maintain good relations with Moscow to ensure they received cheap energy.

Putin shocked the world in 2014. In response to the Ukrainian Revolution, which deposed a pro-Moscow government, he ordered the occupation of Crimea. After this, he indirectly intervened in the Donbas in eastern Ukraine, which resulted in much of this area falling under the control of Moscow loyalists. Moscow believed that it needed to secure Ukrainian territory for its national security.

Vilnius, because of its historical memories, became extremely concerned. Kaliningrad, the Russian exclave, is the home of the Russian Baltic fleet, and from here, Putin's forces could sweep into Lithuania. In 2015, the Baltic fleet conducted a huge exercise off the coast of Lithuania, which was widely seen as an attempt to intimidate the Baltic state. In the same year, Lithuania reintroduced conscription which was reluctantly accepted by the populace.

Since 2014, Lithuania has been in an area of great geopolitical sensitivity. The Suwałki Gap is seen as one of the weak spots of NATO.

This is a thinly populated area on the border of Lithuania and Poland. If this low-lying area is seized by Russia, it would connect Belarus and Kaliningrad and cut off the Baltic states from the rest of Europe. Lithuanians and others, including those involved in NATO, began to fear that Putin would seize the Suwałki Gap. These fears have increased since the president (or dictator) of Belarus, Alexander Lukashenko, became a puppet of Moscow after he stole an election in 2021.

NATO military exercises have been conducted to prepare for any Russian attack on the Suwałki Gap. Many Lithuanians fear another Russian invasion of their land. The Baltic state would not have the forces to repel a large Russian incursion from the Suwałki Gap. The crisis that erupted in 2014 reminded many Lithuanians that they could not take their sovereignty for granted.

Successive Lithuanian governments have actively promoted human rights and the sovereignty of nations. In 2022, Lithuania allowed Taiwan to establish a diplomatic office in the country, which angered the Chinese government since it regards Taiwan as a renegade province. In response to this, Beijing imposed an embargo on Lithuanian exports, which hit many sectors already weakened by the 2020 pandemic. Despite the pressure, Vilnius did not relent.

In 2021, Belarus used migrants to destabilize their neighbors in retaliation for their support of the democratic opposition in Minsk during protests over a stolen election. Belarus, no doubt with the support of Putin, encouraged refugees and illegal migrants to cross their borders into Poland, Lithuania, and other Baltic states. Thousands of migrants poured over the border, and Lithuania created a fence along its border with Belarus. Attempts by migrants to enter led to clashes, and those who did manage to enter the country were usually detained. Some European NGOs (non-governmental organizations) and institutions have criticized the Lithuanian government for its treatment of migrants. Many in Vilnius saw the migrant crisis of 2021 as a form of invasion sponsored by Moscow. The use of migrant flows and cyberattacks is regarded as a form of warfare used by Russia to destabilize the democracies in the Baltic.

Ukraine and Old Fears

In February 2022, the world was shocked by the Russian invasion of Ukraine. Massive formations broke through the borders and headed for Kyiv. Ukraine was able to resist the invaders, and despite heavy losses,

Ukrainians managed to contain the invasion even though they lost territory. Lithuanians became deeply alarmed by this, and they feared that the war would spread to their nation. Russian army units based in Belarus had been deployed during the offensive against Kyiv, and the Suwałki Gap appeared to be their next target. Lithuania strongly supported Kyiv and provided the Ukrainians with arms and financial support.

As Putin's forces became bogged down and after their defeat in the Battle of Kyiv in Ukraine, Lithuania's immediate fears were allayed. Nevertheless, the Baltic republic has started building extensive defenses to protect it from Kaliningrad or Suwałki Gap attacks.

Lithuania has accepted tens of thousands of Ukrainian migrants, and while they have been welcomed, they have placed a tremendous strain on the local society. Many of these are Russian speakers, which has caused further unease. Lithuanian fears over the Russians have increased tensions with the local Russian-speaking minority. They have felt increasingly harassed and excluded from mainstream society. Most of them want to be part of Lithuanian society but also want to keep their language and customs.

Lithuania feels as if it is on the front line of a new cold war. Despite this, the population is committed to maintaining its freedom and has the support of its European and North American allies. Lithuania still feels that it must struggle for its freedom after centuries of war.

Conclusion

Lithuania is a small nation, but it has a long and exciting history. It has had a huge impact on world history. The Lithuanian people are a product of years of war and struggle for freedom. It was the last pagan state in Europe and remained semi-pagan for many years after its Christianization. The Grand Duchy of Lithuania expanded to the east, taking advantage of the failing Mongol Empire. After the union with Poland, Lithuania became joint ruler of the most significant state in eastern Europe. The Grand Duchy of Lithuania became a wealthy and cosmopolitan state. However, it was faced with the growing power of Muscovy, and it became more dependent on Poland. On the face of it, the Grand Duchy of Lithuania remained a European power but was weakened as Russia's power grew. Since the 16th century, Lithuanian history has mainly been defined by the nation's relationship with the Russian giant.

After the Deluge, a series of interconnected wars weakened the Polish-Lithuanian Commonwealth. Lithuanian power was greatly reduced after the Great Northern War. By the late 18th century, Lithuania was a shell of what it had been and became part of the Russian Empire after a series of partitions. This led to over a century of oppression and efforts to destroy the Lithuanian identity.

Lithuania was able to regain its independence after World War I, but it soon collapsed into a dictatorship. Between 1939 and 1945, it was occupied by the Soviet Union, Nazi Germany, and then the Soviet Union again. During this time, the Jewish population was all but exterminated, marking a dark moment in Lithuanian history. In the aftermath of Soviet reoccupation in 1945, the Lithuanian people suffered terribly. By 1991, it regained its independence and once again joined a family of nations.

One of the themes of Lithuanian history is the empire. The Grand Duchy of Lithuania was a huge empire that decisively shaped Eastern Europe and its peoples, such as the Cossacks. Lithuania also played a role in the defeat of empires. One of the reasons Lithuania was able to become an empire was its tolerance of others.

Another theme in Lithuanian history is the struggle for independence and freedom. Since its wars with the Teutonic Knights, the nation has been struggling for freedom and the preservation of its national identity. Lithuania won its freedom, but it still faces an ongoing threat from Russia, especially in the aftermath of the Russo-Ukrainian War. We can only guess what the future holds for Lithuania, but it will likely continue to play an important role in world affairs.

If you enjoyed this book, a review on Amazon would be greatly appreciated because it would mean a lot to hear from you.

To leave a review:
1. Open your camera app.
2. Point your mobile device at the QR code.
3. The review page will appear in your web browser.

Thanks for your support!

Here's another book by Captivating History that you might like

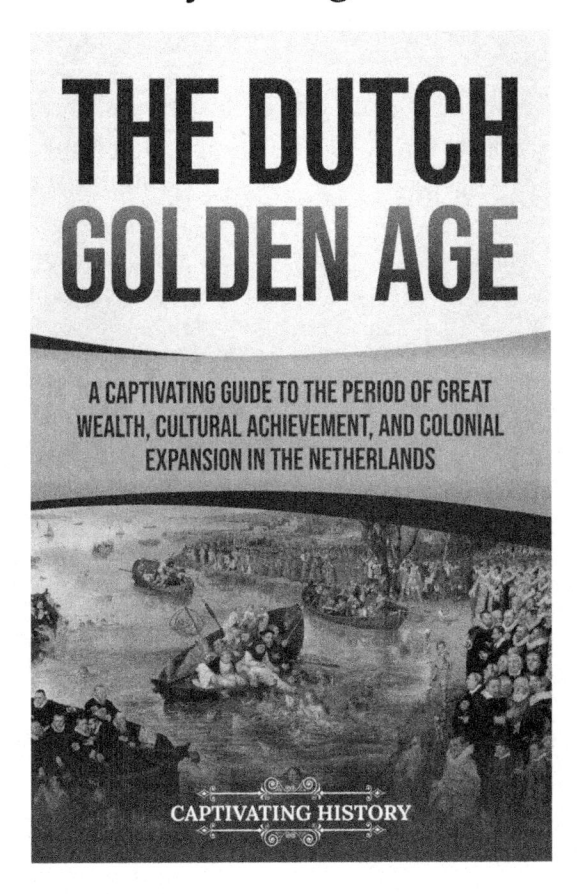

THE DUTCH GOLDEN AGE

A CAPTIVATING GUIDE TO THE PERIOD OF GREAT WEALTH, CULTURAL ACHIEVEMENT, AND COLONIAL EXPANSION IN THE NETHERLANDS

CAPTIVATING HISTORY

Free Bonus from Captivating History (Available for a Limited time)

Hi History Lovers!

Now you have a chance to join our exclusive history list so you can get your first history ebook for free as well as discounts and a potential to get more history books for free!

Simply visit the link below to join.

Or, Scan the QR code!

captivatinghistory.com/ebook

Also, make sure to follow us on Facebook, X, and YouTube by searching for Captivating History.

Bibliography

Eidintas, A., Bumblauskas, A., Kulakauskas, A., Tamošaitis, M., Kondratas, S. and Kondratas, R., 2016. *History of Lithuania*.

Balkelis, T., 2009. *The Making of Modern Lithuania*. Routledge.

Bubnys, A., 2004. "The Holocaust in Lithuania: An Outline of the Major Stages and Their Results." In The vanished world of Lithuanian Jews (pp. 205-221). Brill.

Butterwick, R., 2021. *The Polish-Lithuanian Commonwealth, 1733-1795*. Yale University Press.

Christiansen, E., 1997. *The Northern Crusades (Vol. 927)*. Penguin UK.

Plakans, A., 2011. *A Concise History of the Baltic States*. Cambridge University Press.

Senn, A.E., 1959. *The Emergence of Modern Lithuania*. Columbia University Press.

Jovaiša, E., 2001. "The Balts and Amber." Acta Academiae Artium Vilnensis, 22, pp.149-156.

Vásáry, I., 2016. "Golden Horde Khanate." The Encyclopedia of Empire, pp.1-10.

Mole, R., 2012. *The Baltic States from the Soviet Union to the European Union: Identity, Discourse and Power in the Post-communist Transition of Estonia, Latvia and Lithuania*. Routledge.

Rowell, S.C., 1992. "A Pagan's Word: Lithuanian Diplomatic Procedure 1200-1385." Journal of Medieval History, 18(2), pp.145-160.

Image Sources

[1] MapMaster, CC BY-SA 3.0 <http://creativecommons.org/licenses/by-sa/3.0/>, via Wikimedia Commons; https://commons.wikimedia.org/wiki/File:Baltic_Tribes_c_1200.svg

[2] https://commons.wikimedia.org/wiki/File:Mindo%C5%ADh._%D0%9C%D1%96%D0%BD%D0%B4%D0%BE%D1%9E%D0%B3_(A._Guagnini,_1611).jpg

[3] https://commons.wikimedia.org/wiki/File:Jan_Matejko,_Bitwa_pod_Grunwaldem.jpg

[4] https://commons.wikimedia.org/wiki/File:Autor_nieznany_(malarz_z_kr%C4%99gu_Lukasa_Cranacha_Starszego),_Bitwa_pod_Orsz%C4%85.jpg

[5] https://commons.wikimedia.org/wiki/File:Schultz_John_II_Casimir_Vasa.jpg

[6] https://commons.wikimedia.org/wiki/File:Tartares_lituaniens_en_reconnaissance.jpg

[7] Bundesarchiv, Bild 183-L19427 / Zoll / CC-BY-SA 3.0, CC BY-SA 3.0 DE <https://creativecommons.org/licenses/by-sa/3.0/de/deed.en>, via Wikimedia Commons; https://commons.wikimedia.org/wiki/File:Bundesarchiv_Bild_183-L19427,_Litauen,_brennende_Synagoge.jpg

[8] Rights: Kauno IX forto muziejus / Kaunas 9th Fort Museum, CC BY 4.0 <https://creativecommons.org/licenses/by/4.0>, via Wikimedia Commons; https://commons.wikimedia.org/wiki/File:Lithuanian_deportees_in_Inta_1956.jpeg

[9] Unspecified, GFDL <http://www.gnu.org/copyleft/fdl.html>, via Wikimedia Commons; https://commons.wikimedia.org/wiki/File:January_13_events_in_Vilnius_Lithuania.jpg

[10] Ministry of Defence of the Republic of Lithuania - LAF Land Forces (King Mindaugas hussar battalion), GFDL <http://www.gnu.org/copyleft/fdl.html>, via Wikimedia Commons; https://commons.wikimedia.org/wiki/File:Lithuanian_soldiers_during_combat_training_using_walkie-talkie.jpg

Printed in Great Britain
by Amazon